CAPITOL DAYS

THE STORY OF CARDIFF'S BEST-LOVED CINEMA

T0346975

Tuesday March 16th

AT 8.00pm
(Doors open 7.30pm)

ODEON LEICESTER SQ	NEW VICTORIA (London SW1)	ODEON ILFORD	CAPITOL CARDIFF	ODEON BIRMINGHAM	ODEON MANCHESTER	ODEON Queen St. LEICESTER	ODEON EGLINTON TOLL
TEL: 01-930 6111	TEL: 01-834 5732	TEL: 01-554 2500	TEL: 0222 31316	TEL: 021-643 0615/6	TEL: 061-236 8264/7	TEL: 27603/4	TEL: 041-423 2692
£5.25, £3.15, £2.10	£5.25, £3.15, £2.10	£5.25, £3.15, £2.10	£3.50, £2.50, £1.50	£3.50, £2.50, £1.50	£3.50, £2.50, £1.50	£3.50, £2.50, £1.50	£3.50, £2.50, £1.50

BOX OFFICES OPEN MON-SAT 11.00a.m.-8.00p.m. SUN 4.00p.m.-8.00p.m.

The HEAVYWEIGHT CHAMPIONSHIP of GT. BRITAIN
The BRITISH COMMONWEALTH and EUROPE

SEE IT LIVE! direct from WEMBLEY

Presented by VIEWSPORT LTD

HENRY COOPER CHAMPION

JOE BUGNER Challenger

First come - first served - BOOK NOW!

LOCAL AGENTS:

CARDIFF
BENNY JACOBS 0222 709063
PHIL EDWARDS 0222 37704
CLEOPATRA'S PALACE
0633 62975

MANCHESTER
NAT BASSO
061-740 3998/061-723 3105

GLASGOW
PETER KEENAN 041-427 1622
SPORTSMAN EMPORIUM
041-221 4202
LUMLEYS LTD 041-332 2701

LEICESTER
GEORGE BIDDLES
LEICESTER 62374
JOHNNY GRIFFIN
LEICESTER 29287

BIRMINGHAM
ALEX GRIFFITHS
0902 65377

BAR LICENCES APPLIED FOR

CAPITOL DAYS
THE STORY OF CARDIFF'S BEST-LOVED CINEMA

GARY WHARTON

TEMPUS

Frontispiece: Boxing show at the Capitol

First published 2008

Tempus Publishing
Cirencester Road, Chalford,
Stroud, Gloucestershire, GL6 8PE
www.thehistorypress.co.uk

Tempus Publishing is an imprint of The History Press Ltd

British Library Cataloguing in Publication Data.
A catalogue record for this book is available from the British Library.

ISBN 978 0 7524 4664 6

Typesetting and origination by The History Press Ltd
Printed in Great Britain

Contents

The CAPITOL

CARDIFF'S
Super Cinema
and Café

Programme

EXTERIOR
in Queen Street.
(looking West)

Programme cover, 1920s

one

For the entertainment of the public
— by means of motion pictures

Following the death of Arthur Tilney in 1917, he bequeathed that his considerable shares in the Pavilion and Empire Theatres (Abertillery) Ltd and The Palace Theatre (Ebbw Vale) Ltd be distributed amongst his surviving children Ernest, Harold, Annie, Agnes, Rosa and Mabel. So was the creation of Tilney's Kinemas Ltd, a very prosperous, family-run business predominantly run by Ernest, Harold and Cicely. The company would continue running the Olympia Cinema, Newport, originally opened in May 1913, as well as six other cinemas in Wales, but it arguably reached its zenith with the opening of its own Capitol Super Cinema, Queen Street, Cardiff, on 24 December 1921.

Arthur himself was a man with quite a history in both a business and personal sense. Born in Norfolk in 1843, Arthur was to move to Newport by 1864 after marrying Annie James who a year later gave birth to their first child, Annie. Arthur had spells as a railway stationmaster, clerk, carriage maker and eventually as a timber merchant before his death, aged seventy-four. He was described by the secretary of the Cinema Exhibitors Association, Mr H.V. Davies, as being 'a man fifteen years before his time'. At one point, he operated a roller-skating rink in Abertillery, before ultimately migrating to Newport. Roller skating was then curious pastime that even today periodically drifts back into fashion and many will recall that the old Central Cinema that

TILNEYS KINEMAS LTD.

————————Proprietors————————

CAPITOL, CARDIFF.   OLYMPIA, NEWPORT, Mon.

A. F. DOLMAN, LL.B (Lond.), Managing Director.
C. TILNEY, Director and Secretary

Reply to the Registered Office :

Tilney's Kinemas Ltd letterhead

used to be on the Hayes, in Cardiff, was originally a rink in 1908 before being converted to a full-time picture house in 1911. Arthur purchased a site in Newport which was just next to where the Olympia Cinema would be. The Olympia would later come under the Tilney's Kinemas Ltd banner and was managed by A.R. 'Archie' Tilney, a cousin of Ernest, Harold and Cicely. Archie's name became synonymous with the now-demolished Olympia and prior to this he was also the manager for some five years at two of Arthur's Abertillery cinemas, the Empress and Pavilion. The remaining shares in the Abertillery Pavilion and Empress cinemas, set out in Arthur Tilney's will, were passed down to his six daughters and two sons. Emily and Cicely both had 250 shares, Annie, Rosa and Mabel each had 550 shares and Agnes held 800 shares. It also meant that Ernest was now in possession of a total of 1,300 shares, and Harold, 1,150 shares. Finally, they acquired their father's residue of holdings in the Palace Hall in Ebbw Vale, with 334 shares for Ernest, and Harold, along with Arthur's nephew, James, each holding a total of 333 respectively. Joyce Powis, the daughter of Archie Tilney, who managed the Olympia Cinema in Newport, remembers her uncle Ernest as 'a diddy, little man', someone who possessed a good business brain and whose guidance would steer the family business until his sudden death in 1939. Ernest inherited a considerable legacy from his late father in 1917 and, just as Arthur had done before him, he too left his remaining concerns in Tilney's Kinemas to his immediate family. In Ernest's case, this was his wife Emily, more commonly known as Dorothy, and his adopted daughter, who was also called Joan. He was born in Abertillery, in 1877, and, like all the Tilney children, was considerably short. 'He was a quiet, unruffled man who thought before he spoke,' recounts Mrs Powis. 'One of his sayings about the latest local scandal was "nine days talk, ten days wonder!"' Joan was a close friend of Ernest and Dorothy's daughter and remembers that the family were very wealthy and continued living at the Tilney family home, Druidstone, in St Mellons, Cardiff. Such was their well-being that a small staff was employed to run the day-to-day affairs at the estate. Ernest was always well dressed and was even able to indulge in buying silk suits for their annual summer holidays abroad. Mr C.K. Maidment, of Gabalfa, began working at the Capitol Cinema in 1927, just as Paramount took over the lease of the building from the Tilneys. Ernest and Harold still maintained an office on the top floor of the Capitol during this period and Mr Maidment recollects seeing the brothers around the place, from time to time. Ernest, a 'stout, jolly chap' and Harold, 'slimmer and of a pleasant nature', were regarded by many as being gentleman-like but,

Ernest Tilney

Balcony, 1921

curiously enough, they were not well thought of by some in the local business fraternity. It was even suggested by some that the brothers had a peculiar habit of conducting business deals on the back of cigarette boxes. Whatever the actual truth, with Ernest's death in 1939, the year of the outbreak of the Second World War, his younger brother, Harold, and sister, Cicely, took over the running of Tilney's Kinemas Ltd until Harold's own death in 1948, and to the eventual voluntary liquidation of the company in 1965.

two

The place was like a palace: spacious,
plush and kept in immaculate condition

Julian Dolman, son of Arthur, MD of Tilney's Kinemas Ltd

On 12 March 1919, Ernest Tilney, accompanied by his company solicitor, A.F. Hill, and representatives from Philips & Wride Architects, presented their proposed plans to the city watch committee for the construction of a new venture to be built along Queen Street, tentatively called the Coliseum. As ever, the successful implementation of any such scheme was subject to a number of stringent safety regulations being complied with, and the project was not, upon first submission, passed in its entirety. The City Watch Committee itself voiced no particular objection to the suggested design, to construct a 'cinematograph hall', but it was still necessary for the city engineer being satisfied as to the safety aspects of the installation of a lift within the new building.

Unfortunately, a further watch committee meeting showed that the engineer's communication with the public works committee had decreed the initial Tilney plans as unsatisfactory. Indeed, the public works committee had 'expressed an opinion adverse to the proposed installation of lifts, and on other points'. Item number 1359, 'Coliseum, Cardiff' offered the very first mentioning of a project that would, by October 1921, become known as the

Capitol Cinema, Queen Street, Cardiff. This was due to the fact that it was at this point that A.F. Hill, acting on behalf of his client Ernest Tilney, made an application for both a music and dancing license.

The Capitol's original name, Coliseum, was inspired by the London Coliseum, a huge old variety house built in 1904. This ties together perfectly when we discover that the balcony accoutrements at the Capitol were exact replicas of those found in the Coliseum in London. It seems feasible that the change of name would also have been influenced to some extent by the existence of the Canton Coliseum Cinema, Cowbridge Road, already open since 1913, even though the latter 'Collar' and the Capitol were clearly worlds apart in both scale and appearance. An extensive number of health and safety rules had to be adhered to during this period and they proved to be a constant source of consternation amongst cinema and theatre proprietors within the city.

However, if a continuation of a music, dancing or cinematograph license was to be granted then the strict execution of all such regulations had to be satisfied. There was even an inspection by the theatres sub-committee which, in 1921, visited all existing 'places of entertainment', including the Hippodrome, Queen's Hall and Ninian Cinema to ascertain if any improvements were deemed necessary. If any were, they had to be carried out to enable the owners to continue in business with a renewed license. Mr Robert Redford, manager of the New Theatre, was periodically confronting the watch committee concerning the high costs of having to employ fire officers to be present at each and every performance during a time when profits sometimes proved tight, especially at the Empire and Hippodrome halls.

three

*It is a far, far better thing to say
'I am going to the Capitol' than to say 'I am going to the pictures'*

Capitol advertising slogan from the 1920s

Only the *Western Mail* felt it noteworthy to mention the small but not entirely inconsequential fact that building work had not been fully concluded even on the day the Capitol opened. The amount of construction work still needed could not have been very significant, as the local authorities would never have allowed the Tilneys to open their third cinematic venture if there was much more to do. Open it did, however, at 2.30 p.m., 24 December 1921, with the local press all covering the event on the day or directly following the festive break.

The Capitol was built as a fully fledged theatrical-variety venue and its acoustics once held a revered reputation amongst musicians nationwide. However, the early 1920s was when the cinema in Britain and America was beginning to come in to its own and the decade would march to an average 20 million people taking a trip to the local picture palace each and every week. Perhaps, then, it was quite prudent of the Tilneys to turn the Capitol into Cardiff's latest 'super cinema'. There were already a number of 'places of amusement' in and around Cardiff by 1921, and the city centre in particular was especially well catered for. Centrally, there was Park Hall, boasting

The exterior of the Capitol Cinema, 1921

'special musical interludes by the largest orchestra in Wales', the Cardiff Cinema (opposite Park Place and more commonly known as the Queens), the Pavilion, the Castle ('Facing the castle' as their advertisements used to always say), the Imperial ('Cardiff's superb social centre') and the Central, situated on the Hayes, not to forget the New Theatre and Empire, both of which were presenting a pantomime and play respectively. The Penylan Cinema had the current Jackie Coogan picture and the Gaiety, found along City Road, was also advertising its latest highlights. Many insiders regard the Capitol auditorium as having been built the wrong way around, with its screen not being viewed from the left of the main auditorium, which was where it traditionally would have been positioned. The first projection box was built there on the back girder of the rear wall and its location would continue to cause great consternation to cinema staff there right up to the cinema's eventual closure in 1978. Even in 1921, they appeared to possess a decent sense of humour if what we know to be the truth was, in fact, known then. Take, for example, a report by the *Evening Express*, 'The all-important projection apparatus will be installed ... in a carefully planned room, housing three machines of the latest patent. The public can rest assure that the best brains and experience have been sought to make this part of the business a success'. Dennis Pratt, now working for HTV in Cardiff, was second projectionist at the Capitol from 1957-59 and it was here that he first met his future wife, June, an usherette there from 1959 to 1962. Dennis was employed there during the time when J. Arthur Rank, the cinema's proprietor, installed the second box, allowing for the placing of special projectors needed in 1957, when the Capitol began the screening of the latest wide-screen film, Todd-AO, which was printed on the larger 70mm film stock. To enable this to happen, a second projection box was built directly in front of the old one. This resulted in a hole being knocked through the back of the building to allow access into the theatre auditorium.

Unfortunately for Rank, it was not possible to simply remove the entire wall due to the location of a large carbuncle; a kind of metal skeleton, running through it. The old projection box continued to be used as a rewind room for the new film stock and involved the three projectionists at each shift having to perform the daily ritual of crouching clumsily underneath the older box to reach the new one.

four

The greatest home for pictures and music in Wales

Capitol advertising campaign, 1927

Construction work on the Capitol building was instigated in 1918 by
E. Turner & Sons, Cardiff, from the original architectural plans of another
local firm, Philips & Wride. However, shortly after work had commenced, the
senior partner, John Philips, died, and the plans were extensively redeveloped
by his former assistant, James Barrington Wride, at their Pembroke Terrace
chambers. Curiously, 'Barry' Wride was the youngest student to pass the Royal
Institute of British Architects (RIBA) examinations when he qualified as an
architect. It is commonly known that there are a number of idiosyncrasies
within the design of the Capitol, and one ponders as to whether or not this
was a result of the scheme mirroring the psyche of its architect.

This bode well enough for an interesting scenario, but it is more likely the
case that the peculiarities in the plans were influenced by external constraints,
such as the Tilneys inability to acquire the freehold to a selection of slum
properties, a cul-de-sac, directly behind the building.

E. Turner & Sons was a business started by Ephraim Turner in 1885, and the
company was responsible for the construction of many landmark buildings
in Cardiff; including the City Law courts, the old Central Library and Duke
Street and Morgan Arcades. Ephraim passed away in 1912, after having retired
in 1896, and his family contributed enormously to Cardiff, with his original

Right: Portrait of James Turner, the builder responsible for the erection of the Capitol building

Below: Capitol Theatre logo banner

company still in existence today as E.Turner & Sons Construction, now based in Cathedral Road, Cardiff.

Capitol Trailers

The Capitol was the first cinema to introduce the ice-cream covered cone – known originally as a parfait during the run of *The Sound of Music* in the mid-1960s. The Capitol also the first usage of microwave machines for heating hot dogs & beef burgers. (Marcella Dutton, Capitol Cinema worker for almost forty years)

five

Capitol Service, Sir!

Capitol advertising slogan from the 1920s

With parts of its concrete floors still in the process of drying out, Christmas Eve 1921 marked the official inauguration of the Capitol Super Cinema, Queen Street, Tilney's Kinemas first Cardiff-based cinema. 'The Cap', as most local people would come to know it, on that day became the largest cinema in Wales and one of the biggest in the country with its special, invitation-only charity performance. As the 2.30 p.m. opening time came ever closer, building work had been continuing at a furious pace, both night and day. Scaffolding around its exterior had virtually ingrained itself into the general landscape of Queen Street, and its subsequent removal raised a great deal of interest amongst Cardiffians.

Meanwhile, within the Capitol itself, chaos was ensuing as last-minute preparations were concluded not just to facilitate the benefit show, but to meet the deadline for a second important event: a 6 p.m. opening to the general public. This was when local people could at last catch their first glimpse of the luxurious interior. Reinforced concrete was used for the structure of the building due to the diversion of materials and skilled labour for the erection of new homes fit for returning compatriots of the First World War. Therefore, the Capitol had the honour, by default, of being the largest building in the city to use concrete as its main ingredient, primarily because it required less skilled labour as its main concern. 'One of the most interesting features,' accorded the now-defunct *Evening Express*, 'is that it is practically free from wood. This is most essential for this class of building,' This was not completely accurate, as an oak-block floor was laid in the basement cafe (later used as a dancehall) along with Austrian oak panelling on its walls, whilst in comparison the floors on the remaining four storeys were finished in cement with either a 'hygienic' linoleum or carpet base. The main entrance measured a width of 69ft x a depth of 92ft, in front of which stood two resplendent commissionaires clad in peaked caps, full-length coats and striped trousers with a gold-braid edging. Both would stand outside, from mid-morning right through to late evening, beckoning passers-by to come inside. Working hours were both long and arduous but, despite this, many people that worked at 'the Cap' over the years spoke of the warmth of the working environment. Visitors walking through the two vestibules and past both pay boxes were led to a staircase leading to a sprawling lounge area and onto the balcony. Even if you only visited the Capitol once, almost everyone remembers the stairwell as being an integral feature of the building. 'There was a beautiful staircase with a gorgeous brass handrail, leading from the foyer to the restaurant and circle', recounts Mrs Elsie Dowding (née Howard), a Capitol usherette from 1937-39. 'Everything was so spotless, it was all so eye catching – you felt good just walking in there to see a show.'

If patrons did not want to walk to the first floor, newly installed and safety certified, electrical lifts could convey you to any part of the theatre 'with a minimum effort'. Pay boxes were positioned at either side of the main entrance offering 3d and 6d tickets for the cheaper seats and 1s 3d, 1s 6d and 2s 4d for the remainder. Some time later, admission would increase to 1s 9d, 2s 9d or 3s 9d for balcony seats. The very latest high-speed, electronic ticket machines were used at the Capitol to deal efficiently with the vast number of eager cinemagoers. Fact fans will be interested to know that this patented machine was the first of its kind to be fast and efficient and there were even differing selections of change accessible to cashiers to give change from whatever the total cost of tickets purchased proved to be.

'The Capitol was a lovely cinema,' remembers Mrs M. Lewis of Whitchurch, Cardiff. 'After the flight of steps, there was a deep, plush red carpet in the foyer, which your feet sank into. The ushers always greeted patrons as they entered. Even the manager was shaking hands with everyone before we went in, wishing everybody a good evening.' This was the Capitol effect upon one early visitor. The Cardiff press were also gushing in their praise. The *Evening Express* exclaimed, 'Of the splendour of the theatre it would be difficult to speak in terms of exaggeration', whilst the *South Wales Echo* also voiced their opinion that, 'As a cinema it is indeed a Super one'.

A total seating capacity of a little over 3,000 was incorporated into the theatre; 2,078 in the stalls and 1,080 in the gallery (balcony). In addition to this, space for a further 500 people could be made available, should the need arise. The ceiling and side walls were tastefully decorated with plaster and mouldings exemplifying the in-house style, 'lending the whole entrance the seal of artistic effectiveness.' Eva Patterson, now in her eighties, was employed to work in the first-floor restaurant and to this day she can still vividly recall the murals painted over the walls there. An artist, Mr Barnes, was responsible for the artwork, and Eva recollects being struck by the beauty of one particular design. It pictured a ballerina. She and her two sisters worked there when, just like the usherettes, staff would be subjected to a daily 'parade' to check personal hygiene and cleanliness prior to opening. This was when a coffee at the Capitol cost 6d and a tram, in the city centre, was a mere 2d.

In keeping with the American ideal for sprawling, gravity-confounding auditoriums, built to a vast scale, the balcony at the Capitol was unusual in that it was entirely free of restrictive supporting pillars. This meant that patrons could be certain of a clear, unimpeded view of the screen and stage below. It is worth noting that this cannot be said for the newer Cardiff International Arena. Each and every row of seating in the balcony was of an American variety; single, tip-up arm chairs with an 'additional amenity of shelves at the back of all seats.' They were regarded as being especially spacious and convenient, allowing other patrons to remain seated should someone else wish to pass along their row; an inconvenience frequently incurred by modern cinema visitors. Sadly, in later years they would be left in a dilapidated state: unkempt, and rotting away. Reproductions for the plaster works to add to the already existing visual aesthetic were also included.

Pillar inside the Capitol

Another distinctive quality of the auditorium was its wonderful oval ceiling, forming the base of a dome. Vaguely reminiscent of Brunelleschi's cathedral in Florence, to the novice anyway, it dominated the building at a height of 15ft from the top of the balcony. A total of twelve separate members would spring forth, forming an oval ring that in itself was overshadowed by a smaller dome. Decorated in a Greek key pattern, plastic decorations with heraldic shields and fleur-de-lys were embodied upon a shield of deep red. Complemented by a chiselled Bathstone tapering in the ceiling, the 'whole combination [was] at once pleasing, original and effective'.

Returning back downstairs and into the main auditorium via the staircase or using one of the lifts, patrons arrived back into the heart of the theatre, measuring an imposing 138ft x 116ft square. It was here that an extensive number of rows of circularly arranged seats were built. During the period when most adults and quite a number of young adults smoked heavily, the cupola roof at the Capitol would be opened, weather permitting. Only the Penylan (later known as the Globe Cinema), in Roath, had a similar quirk to

The balcony in the Capitol Cinema

its functional architecture. However, at the Penylan it would take two people to wind the roof shut if a sudden downpour occurred. Gas heating and hot-water radiators were considered for use in the auditorium but rejected in favour of the incorporation of a suitable system of steam radiators to warm and project 'fresh clean air' into the cinema. These were chosen and situated around the building, from whence it was possible to control its temperature from the boiler house and either heat or cool it within a five-minute period. The space used for housing the boiler was rumoured to be a former synagogue prior to its extensive life as the centre point of the heating system at the Capitol. A huge fan, driven by a 14hp motor, would draw in heat from outside the cinema and through the radiators, forcing it past a number of air cleaners and humidifiers to the preferred degree requested. The air was then passed through huge ducts in the floor and eventually into the auditorium itself by way of 100 specially constructed grids, set into to the aisle floor. The Tilneys hoped to eliminate all possibilities of draughts and to allow their patrons the uppermost in comfort. Customer contentment was what 'Capitol service, sir!' was all about and even the *South Wales Echo* proclaimed that indeed, there was 'ample provision for the admission of light and air to the building'. Such was the nature of the time, it was reported that the whole place was fire proof! What was regarded a highly reliable heating system in 1921, would produce annoyance to future decades of audiences and performers at the Capitol, with the idiosyncratic cranking of pipes proving a consistent source of irritation. On the final night, in January 1978, the dreaded pipes would screech their last desperate gasp of breath after the final film performance played to a sparse audience.

Seating in all the 1,080 possible positions in the auditorium was composed of heavily upholstered silk, stuffed with treated horsehair and arranged in three main bays, allowing for four aisles of considerable width and convenience. Unlike the majority of cinemas in Cardiff, the floor at the Capitol was not stepped in the usual manner but consisted of each row of seats being 3in higher than the one before it. Quaintly, this meant that everybody could see the screen clearly 'without the necessity for ladies having to remove their hats for people sitting behind to be able to see without interruption.' Tilney's Kinemas wanted to keep the price of admission competitive and their intention was to allow for a considerable number of patrons to be able to visit the Capitol rather than to limit themselves with a higher admission cost and smaller audiences. Ironically, some years later such an immense auditorium would prove almost impossible to fill, unless a major hit film in the ilk of a James Bond, was presented there. Otherwise, seats were always available for all performances.

Mr H.V. Davies, secretary of the Cinematograph Exhibitors' Association, performed the opening ceremony at the cinema and was highly complimentary of the Tilneys, whom he was to comment, 'were not in the business merely to make money, but were actuated by ideals'. The programme for that day began with a rendering of Offenbach's *Orpheus in the Underworld,* followed by a brief speech from Mr Davies, the highlight of which was the following revelation: 'When the cinema is complete, it will be a centre of many phases of the life of the Cardiff community.' This basically meant that anyone could afford the price of a ticket.

Yet, considering the scale of the building and its embracing of electrical lifts (to the gallery and cafés), ladies and gents hairdressing salons, cafés, rest rooms, kitchens, cloakrooms and tea lounge, it comes as no great surprise that it as not completely finished. 'What is it?' asked a newspaper advertisement to promote the new cinema. The question was a rhetorical one and an answer was forthcoming: 'The Capitol is the latest development in the evolution of the cinema.' Indeed, there was nothing quite like the Capitol Theatre anywhere else in Cardiff or even the Principality in 1921 and expectations were high: 'Messrs Tilneys undertake to maintain the high standards set ... and therefore there is no room for two options as to the success of this remarkable enterprise of theirs,' exclaimed the *Evening Express* concluding: 'A magnificent theatre in which only the best pictures are shown ... [it] cannot but be a success in a city like Cardiff.'

What was not reported was the little-known fact that the electricians responsible for fitting out the Capitol had a major disagreement with the management, resulting in the cessation of their work. It was left to the formidable Cicely Tilney to actually connect the remaining circuits herself and the opening day proceeded without further problems.

The latest edition of *Eve's Film Review*, an early kind of screen magazine directed at a female audience, followed. The magazine ran throughout the 1920s and 1930s, and was deemed of 'special interest for the ladies'.

A violin solo of Chopin's *Sonsati* from Lionel Falkman, the orchestra leader at the Capitol. The Park Hall had Garforth Mortimer, Lindsey Priest was at the Queen's and the Capitol Orchestra was led by the aforementioned Mr Falkman. Described as a 'moustachioed, bespectacled man,' Falkman's newly formed, twelve-piece orchestra performed prior to the screening of the main feature. Fresh from the Royal Opera, Covent Garden, Lionel was a laudable musician in South Wales and Newport; being at one time the leading violinist in an orchestra fronted by Arthur Angle.

Mr Falkman's reputation did not go undetected by the press covering the events on the day. The *Western Mail* had nothing but praise, 'As a violinist he is a genius, as a conductor he has very high gifts and under his direction the music provided at the Capitol will be of rare quality'. The newspaper was just as fulsome in its praise about his solo recital, 'the rendering of which night is Capitol night'. The first significant feature film to play at the Capitol was the British-produced *Nothing Else Matters* (1927). Of importance in 1921 was the advocacy of presenting British films and the Tilneys vocalised their support of this. In fact, although they did promise to show British-made films at the Capitol, the reality was that, even in the early 1920s, Hollywood and the major American film studios were wholly dominant in both the British and American market place. Still, *Nothing Else Matters* was outlined as 'a picture which tells a good story and is full of incident and of character. It gained unanimous and enthusiastic appreciation ... and this afternoon's audience endorsed unmistakably that judgement.' The pro-Brit Capitol soon reverted back to showing the latest American films a little time later, with a combination of educational, scientific and cartoon pictures in support.

Capitol Trailers

Two trained nurses are on duty each evening in the theatre. Will medical gentlemen please inform ushers the position of their seats so they may be called in the event of any messages arriving for them. (Theatre programme note)

six

We were the best and we knew it

C.J. Burke, Paramount/Capitol pageboy

In the spring of 1926, Western Electric and Warner Brothers joined together to form the Vitaphone Corporation, with the intention of producing and marketing talking pictures. The canny brothers Warner realized that theatres would need to extensively re-equip their auditoriums to allow this new and exciting development to be presented to the public. Therefore, the production studio developed the necessary hardware required to enable this to happen and thus reap the ensuing financial rewards. Their first joint venture was the 1926 release *Don Juan*, co-starring John Barrymore and Mary Astor. The film contained a synchronized musical score throughout, coupled with added sound effects, and it proved to be a great popular success amongst audiences.

Don Juan would arrive at the Queen's Super cinema, Queen Street, in July of the following year and also went on to play the Pavilion Cinema, and the Plaza in Gabalfa, Cardiff by 1928. It was the public response to the new sound system which convinced the major film studios that talking pictures were the future for the industry. Hesitation and doubts had been rife amongst certain studios and cinema exhibitors due to the massive and costly task that would have to be undertaken to install the new system. The feelings amongst the American media were distinctly conciliatory: 'Vitaphone will get 'em,'

Vitaphone sound advertisement

proclaimed *Variety*, 'Men, women and children. It's the unprecedented success of filmville,' A man named Al was shortly to change the course of film history but, wait a moment, there's more to come before we meet that particular gentleman.

The Lodger (1926), an early Alfred Hitchcock film starring local hero Ivor Novello, had played at the Capitol in April 1927, but the most significant news for the cinema was the closure of its rival the Queen's in early June. This was in readiness for its own subsequent September relaunch as the 'cosiest and finest appointed Super cinema in the principality.' In July, the heralding of the *Echo* headline 'Newcastle magnate buys Cardiff cinema' also reported that the lease to the Capitol had been purchased by Mr Issac 'Ike' Collins.

Mr Collins was a well-known northern businessman at the time and had made his fortune in the public amusements area. It was noted that former leaseholders Tilney's Kinemas Ltd had offered the sale of the lease for a considerable period prior to its eventual purchase by Mr Collins on Monday, 1 August. There was to be no booming declaration by the new owners or about Paramount's involvement with the Capitol in any of the daily programme listings in the local press. Enthusiasm was a-plenty in the weekly film listings for the Capitol, urging Cardiffians about the merits of 'The greatest programme yet ... a programme to please ... the greatest entertainment in the principality,' and finally of 'a programme not to be missed'. Such indications of an American involvement only became apparent upon analyzing the features shown after this period, one being titled *Fascinating Youth*, with 'Paramount's junior stars presented at the theatre.

Across the city, the Playhouse Theatre (known later as the Gala Cinema), offered *Cinderella* for its festive season, whilst Tom Jones and his famous Queen's Orchestra was a popular act at the Queen's Cinema, in an already congested central area already containing the Park Hall and Olympia. Lionel Falkman remained as the Capitol's resident orchestra leader, now billed as being 'with his augmented Classical Jazz orchestra,' performing with a host of other guests announced as 'another charming interlude ... Capitol frolics'. The Tilney brothers retained their offices on the top floor of the theatre.

Meanwhile, a new managerial strategy was instigated almost immediately. Paramount now began to develop the theatre, showing mainly feature films

CAPITOL

SUNDAY NOVEMBER 15th for 6 days

CHARLTON HESTON in
"MASTER OF THE ISLANDS"

co-starring **GERALDINE CHAPLIN**
JOHN PHILLIP LAW   MAKO
also starring **TINA CHEN** as 'Nyuk Tsin'
ALEC McCOWEN as 'Micah Hale'

also HELL BOATS

Charlton Heston, 1970s

Cardiff Municipal Musical Society

PRESENTS

Grand Concert

AT THE

CAPITOL   THEATRE,   CARDIFF

(By kind permission of C.R.A.)

SUNDAY, JANUARY 16th, 1949.   **2.45 p.m.**

CARDIFF MUNICIPAL MUSICAL SOCIETY

B.B.C. WELSH ORCHESTRA (*Augmented*)

(*Leader* : PHILLIP WHITEWAY)

ISOBEL BAILLIE (*Soprano*)

ROWLAND JONES (*Tenor*)

(By permission of Governors, Sadlers Wells)

Conductor   -   MANSEL THOMAS

(*Accompanist to Society*   -   -   CEINWEN PARKER, L.R.A.M.)

Programme   -   -   -   -   -   -   -   *THREEPENCE*

Capitol concert cover for the Cardiff Municipal Musical Society, 1949 for the then mighty studio from that point on. It was during the 1920s that the studio attained its golden age with stars such as Clara Bow, Gloria Swanson and Rudolph Valentino combining to provide a dynamic set of box-office attractions. In 1927, the year that Len Davies scored the winning goal for Cardiff City in the FA Cup final, Paramount saw their talents reach a crescendo with the best picture Academy Award for the aerial adventure *Wings*. 'You will soon hear the whir of "Wings," "Wings," "Wings," roared the Capitol advertisements: strangely enough, though, this Clara Bow feature was a silent release! 'We were the smartest cinema in Cardiff and we knew it,' vaunts Mr C.J. Burke of Llanedeyrn, a pageboy at the Cap' in the early 1930s.

With its fountain playing in the main foyer, the usherettes were colourfully dressed in the company livery of a loose, dark-blue blouse with a large golden bow in the front, complemented by cream trousers. A concerted reinvestment of staff was established by Paramount and the new manager, A.E. Warren, had been poached from the Plaza Theatre in London. Dressed in full evening attire, Mr Warren and his house manager, also immaculately costumed in a tuxedo, would greet cinemagoers as they entered the cinema.

With that, the scene was set for the next chapter in the elongated history of the Capitol Cinema. Mr C.K. Maidment, from whom we have already heard, worked firstly as a pageboy and then as an assistant electrician from the time that Paramount took over through to 1939. He met and married his wife, who was working in the restaurant, during his employment there. His memories are therefore fond ones, 'Everyone was so helpful and you could have a meal or refreshment before going into the cinema.' In the early 1930s, the uniformed staff was made up of three or four commissionaires, six pageboys and around fifteen usherettes, the pageboys wearing light blue with a wide contrasting stripe down the side of the trousers, a stiff shirt front and winged collars with a white bow tie. The commissionaires wore dark-blue trousers and peaked caps with accompanying long coats, fine for the colder months but cumbersome in the summertime.

Back to Mr Maidment. 'The show was always first class; two features, news, forthcoming attractions, a comedy and a stage show. There were always trams and buses waiting outside, (this was during the pre-pedestrianised Queen Street days) for patrons living on the outskirts of the city.' A packet of ten

Above: Capitol commissionaires/pageboys, 1920s

Opposite: Usherettes, 1937

Usherettes, post-war

cigarettes typically cost 5d, and adverts selling Palmolive soap entreated consumers to 'keep the schoolgirl complexion' by simply purchasing the 6d product enhancing or sustaining 'the beauty that men admire!' Quaint, or just plain condescending? The choice is yours.

'It was a magnificent building and we were a very popular cinema indeed, with evening performances finding the cinema full, with waiting queues,' reminisced Mr C.J. Burke, another former Capitol pageboy. 'The Capitol had a peculiar arrangement inside the auditorium, whereby, on the right side, ran a wooden partition right down the length of the theatre with a drop-bar at the screen end. This was used for patrons who had bought the cheapest tickets for the front stalls, and they had to stand there (because the Capitol had a policy of continuous performances) until the usherettes could find empty seats.'

A particularly amusing tale concerned cinemagoer Bernard O'Sullivan, one person who waited in line, which occurred some years later. As I included in my previous book, *Ribbon of Dreams: Remembering the Cardiff Cinemas*, the American actor Charlton Heston visited the Capitol at least twice, as part of film promotional tours. He came to the theatre in 1953 for a screening of *The Greatest Show on Earth* (1952). Bernard tells the story:

I had to stand at the back of the cinema, waiting for any vacant seats, when the fellow next to me, quite a big chap, was at the back next to the aisle. I was next in line for a seat and he was next after me. We exchanged a few words about having to wait and he agreed. The next thing the lights went up before the film started, and the manager said a few words, 'and now I will introduce the star of the show – Mr Charlton Heston,' and this big fellow I had been talking with, patted me on the shoulder and walked on to the stage – it was him!

Another visit paid by Mr Heston during the 1960s set the scene shortly after he had been introduced to the audience by the ever-present manager, Bill Hall. Heston wanted to hear the crowd sing, as he had been informed that the Welsh were known for their wonderful singing voices. 'I was floored, I didn't know what to do,' blushed Mr Hall, remembering the incident in an *Echo* interview. 'I asked everyone to join me in Sospan Fach. I sang it alone, 2500 people out there and me on the stage ... I prayed the floor would eat me up.' Strangely enough, the incident was not one included in the autobiography written by Mr Heston and published a few years ago. I cannot imagine why not.

Also of interest, on 5 September, was the opening of the Coliseum Cinema, or 'Collar' as it was more commonly known. This former theatre in Cowbridge road, Canton, had been in use as a cinema since 1913 and now came under the control of the Carreras' Cinema Circuit. By November, in addition to the Collar, they took charge of the Penylan Cinema, Albany road, itself known as the Globe Cinema to most people. Willie Foxhall was made the leader of the in-house orchestra at the Coliseum, after it was publicly announced by the management as now being 'one of the cosiest cinemas in Cardiff', the significance of which meant it was a small auditorium.

As the end of the year approached the promise of 'colossal entertainment' offered by cinemas such as the Capitol began to have an enormous effect upon city centre theatres. Audiences had been declining since the days of the war years, where money was oddly aplenty, and now theatre proprietors remonstrated that three hours of cinematic amusement by popular stars of the day proved more enticing than stage productions often at half this length, and mostly twice or triple the 1s cinema admission charge.

seven

Friday night is 'Capitol' night

Capitol advertising slogan, 1929

Audiences at the Park Hall Cinema could, in January 1928, have their breath taken away for the price of a 1-2s as Ramon Navarro roared across the silver screen as the definitive *Ben Hur* (1925). Collectively, cinemas in Cardiff adopted a different advertising slogan almost every week in an attempt at enticing filmgoers to see the current releases. Lionel Falkman and his Capitol Jazzmaniacs band were in print as 'the rage of Cardiff' during the period which found the jazz style very much in vogue. Meanwhile, over at the Queen's Cinema, Lindsey Priest and his orchestra endeavoured to satisfy the in-house adverting assertion that promised they could play as succinctly as a record, whilst in March and October, Tom Jenkins and his '10 Plazaites' and the Archie Roberts Orchestra, at the Plaza and Regent cinemas respectively, took their places alongside a broadening ensemble of musicians enhancing the flickering image at picture houses all around town.

A fresh style of press advertisements promoting the Capitol Cinema featured two usherettes holding bold "CAPITOL" letters on either side, and dressed in their popular uniforms topped off with large, golden bows. However, commonly, the new logo was to be used inconsistently and soon disappeared from subsequent ads.

Friday evenings at the Capitol arguably offered the best value for money to audiences, as in addition to the usual programme, a 'Capitol night' provided Paramount comedies, news and musical interludes, supplied in this case by the nimble-fingered Mr Falkman and Co. Weekend amusements concluded with admission to Sunday concerts at the Capitol ranging from 1s 3d, 1s 6d and 2s 4d. This was in a year that saw cinema attendances nationally at 25.2 million.

The Imperial Picture Palace, which would regenerate as the Queen Street Odeon by 1936, unlocked its doors for a second time, after a substantial period of closure, with not the most exciting of features, *The Price of Ignorance*. Billed as a 'public sermon' warning of the perils of ignorance, it remained unclear what sort of ignorance was being warned against, but one assumes that cinemagoers were enlightened after attending either of the segregated, male or female screenings. Contemporary audiences would have stayed away in droves at this documentary film, which resurfaced for an additional run at the Queen's Cinema in June.

Eccentric pontificating prevailed throughout Cardiff cinemas in 1928, with the newly-opened Plaza Cinema, found on North road, joining the melee, albeit rhetorically. 'If you desire to know,' read the press ads, 'visit the Plaza.' On 22 October, the Regent Super Cinema, Ely, became the latest in the burgeoning Splott Circuit portfolio. Its first big feature presentation was Ivor Novello in *The Constant Nymph* (1928). It had already played at the Capitol but, nonetheless, the local community flocked to the opening night, paying between 6d and 1s 3d.

eight

Wait a minute, wait a minute. You ain't heard nothing yet!

Al Jolson in The Jazz Singer

The second week of February 1929 saw the first Cardiff viewing of the Al Jolson musical *The Jazz Singer* (1927) at the Capitol, in twelve months that proved to be of major importance for cinemas in the city. An advertisement in the *Echo*, placed at the beginning of the month, excitingly teased the public of what was on its way, 'Coming: The picture which created the great 'talkie' sensation'. The film arrived on 11 February, supported by a W.C. Fields comedy, but there was no overt public mention of the inclusion of sound.

Remaining in that month, the Queen's Super Cinema adopted a straightforward campaign: 'Watch carefully ... this will be the first up-to-date talkie programme in Wales ... See and Hear Al Jolson in *The Singing Fool*'. It was the Capitol's rival, the Queen's, premiering of *The Singing Fool* (1928) on 9 March, that cemented the arrival of the new 'talkies' sensation in Wales and it remained there until May. However, even this, Jolson's second film for the Warner studio, only contained a few scenes of dialogue and was mainly a silent picture, with similar musical accompaniment to that found in *The Jazz Singer*. Leslie Halliwell, the late British film critic, defined *The Singing Fool* as 'a pretty maudlin piece of drama' (Halliwell's *Film & Video Guide*, 1988 edition). *The Jazz Singer* is often erroneously cited as being the first talkie but it only contained segments of improvised dialogue and musical interludes, such as

Right and below: Al Jolson in *The Jazz Singer* (1927)

Sonny Boy. It was the effect of the infamous Jolson speech, 'Wait a minute, wait a minute. You ain't heard nothin' yet! Wait a minute, I tell you. You ain't heard nothin yet', that generated the impression that a real conversation was taking place on screen that pulled audiences into the heart of the film. Jolson was known as the world's greatest entertainer and even though he was not revered

Al Jolson in *The Jazz Singer* (1927)

for his acting talents, it was his sheer force of personality that made the film the biggest box-office success of its day until being overtaken by the release of *Gone with the Wind* in 1939.

Whilst audiences across at the Queen's Cinema were enthralled with the sounds of Jolson for 1s 2d or 2s, the Capitol remained silent until the interest of film fans was titillated by the notification of the arrival of their first '100% talkie' being imminent: 'Next week listen to ... a revolution in cinema entertainment ... listen to the screen's most outspoken confession'. *The Doctor's Secret* (1928) was to be the first talking picture released by Paramount, and during its brief run at the Capitol from 6 May, it was supported by a silent picture, *Just Married* (1927). On the Capitol stage, soprano Sylvia Robbins was accompanied by Falkman and his orchestra, coming together for one of the popular Friday-night shows, enhancing an already exceedingly fine programme consisting of continuous films playing four times a day.

By the same token, the Queen's Cinema was heavily advertising itself as 'Cardiff's Talking Picture Theatre' and during the same period it was itself showing *On Trial* (1928), which, of course, went on to be screened at the Pavilion Cinema in July of that same year. Economically priced train tickets were made available by Great Western Railways to entice film fans into making the journey down from areas including the Rhondda Valley, Aberdare, Bridgend and Merthyr. A regional newspaper review of *On Trial* was plain in its analysis, 'All these people have wonderful speaking voices'. Competition was silent from local rivals like the Park Hall, Gaiety, Plaza and Regent Cinemas, but the effect of *The Doctor's Secret* and other talking pictures upon the remaining variety houses within the central area of Cardiff was becoming apparent. Moss Empires, owners of the Empire Theatre on Queen Street, a few doors up from the Imperial and Olympia cinemas (ABC & Odeon) was hedging its bets by wiring its theatres for talkies, 'it is not accurate to say that talking pictures are killing the ordinary theatre,' said a spokesperson. 'Talking theatres are having lean weeks just as we are: the thing is to prepare for any development.' Still, by 11 May the Capitol was back to screening 'silents', with Fay Wray and Gary Cooper starring in *The Legion of the Condemned* (1927) and, from this point on, the Capitol adopted a programming policy which mixed both 'silents' and 'talkies'.

THE WORLD'S GREATEST ENTERTAINER

AL JOLSON

In his greatest Singing triumph—an absorbing Love Story
"THE SINGING FOOL"
Commg: SATURDAY APRIL 26th at the
EXCELSIOR THEATRE

Above: Capitol 'Talkies' advertisement

Left: Al Jolson in *The Singing Fool* (1928) poster

By the end of May, the Capitol began a new style of advertising to attract custom: exasperation. 'At last! The perfect talking picture – *The Donovan Affair*.' Forthcoming attractions introduced the latest film to star Ruth Chatterton, the star of Paramount's *The Doctor's Secret*, in her second talking picture *The Dummy*, whereby 'the whole cast speaks'. *The Singing Fool* returned for a second stint in Cardiff, this time singing its way onto the screen at the Pavilion. Situated on St Mary's Street, the Pavilion had been featuring both 'silents' and 'talkies' when *The Singing Fool* arrived there on 10 June.

Sound pictures had quashed all that had come before them and their grip upon the industry was becoming voracious. In July, the proclamations at the Capitol were unrelenting in pursuit of its film presentations, 'The triumph of the talkies ... All singing! All playing! All dancing! – Syncopation'. There was still more to come, 'Alluring girls! Gloriously dressed! Dazzling scenes!' As the decade gave way for a new one, the 'revolution in cinema entertainment' continued to increase annual admissions whilst the country moved in to what would be an uncertain present – the 1930s.

nine

Where all dancers are assured of a jolly evening

A 1953 advertisement promoting the Capitol dancehall

Beginning its commercial life as one of the three original cafés within the theatre, the basement area of the Capitol Theatre had a staircase leading down to it on the right side of its Queen Street entrance. It was also accessible from within the main theatre and, measuring 82ft x 50ft, was to be most fondly remembered as the best dancehall venue in the city. Known originally as the Caberet, local people held it in high esteem because the Capitol was different – it had its own band called the Capitol Orpheans, and was head and shoulders above its competitors, most of which were little more than glorified village halls.

The main staircase proved to be the gateway to paradise for one young boy, Stan Philips, who used it as his own private entrance for getting in for free. Stan explains:

When I was sure that the doorman wasn't looking, down the stairs I would rush. Once at the bottom, it was a simple matter of creeping along the corridor past the studio. At the end and to the left was a short flight of steps. This found me at an emergency exit door (never locked) and, once through this, I was behind a curtain. Peeping through this, I could watch out for any usherettes, before creeping off to my chosen seat. At this time I was around ten or eleven, and had ways of getting into all the Queen Street cinemas without paying. It was wrong of course, but it was always fun to do.

In the course of the war years and a little after, the dancehall was operated by a Jewish gentleman, Koppel Lermon, and his brother. Admission cost 5s and once inside this was where you stayed unless you were prepared to pay an additional 5s to come back in again. In these years it garnered a reputation as a notoriously popular meeting place for American servicemen to jitterbug with the local girls and was nicknamed in the locality as the 'bad apple.' The dance hall was controlled by a succession of people, including Miss Peggy Smith, Victor Silvester and Dennis and Brenda Howells. Miss Smith also gave dancing lessons and she eventually married Sam Lewis, an under manager at the Capitol. Dennis Howells arrived at the Capitol in the 1950s as a dance teacher, and along with Brenda, taught some 100,000 people to mouth aloud, '1-2-3-4 ... 1-2-3-4'.

In September 1953, the Capitol Ballroom reopened, with the price of seats upstairs in the cinema costing 4s, 3s 1d and 2s 3d. Late buses were provided so that patrons could get back home after an evening spent in the company of

Capitol Café interior, 1921

★ **CAPITOL CAFE** ★

ALWAYS " AT YOUR SERVICE."

 FOR MORNING COFFEE

VARIED LUNCHEONS   TEAS

IN PLEASANT AND COMFORTABLE SURROUNDINGS

Capitol Café advertisement

Locarno's Dance Orchestra at 'Cardiff's finest dance venue where all dancers are assured of a jolly evening'. Enthusiasts could also have paid a visit to any of the three other halls in Cardiff, including the Pavlova on Leckwith Road or the Louis Ballroom in St Mary Street. It was in the course of the mid-1950s that Rank and Victor Silvester joined forces in launching a chain of dance studios named after the performer, which often or not would be in place of former restaurant areas. This was demonstrative of the willingness by Rank to allow cinemas to be used for purposes other than solely as film venues, prior to the halls being sold off completely.

ten

After the performance visit the Capitol cafe.
The brightest and most cheerful in the city.

Capitol slogan from the 1920s

Remaining in the late 1920s, Ethel Richards, of Llanishen, began working at the Capitol as a cashier, shortly after Paramount took over the lease. 'The walls in the restaurant were hand painted and were generally admired,' she now recalls. Coincidentally, Eva Patterson was also working in the buttery around this time and she mentions that there were two ladies who combined to play as part of the restaurant band prior to the outbreak of the Second World War. One of them was called Dolly Allen, whose parents owned a music shop in City Road. Mrs Richards explains:

The restaurant was always packed in the evenings, 'especially with teenagers who liked to listen to the orchestra and hoped to meet the band. I met my late husband when I worked at the Cap. He was the trumpet player. Unfortunately when the Talkies came, all the cinema orchestras were put out of work. Lionel Falkman went to London and formed a band for one of the Lyons corner houses. Wally Bishop, another band member, formed his own band which my husband. They went touring as the very popular Waldini's Gypsy Band.

Capitol stairway

Mrs B. Darcy of Roath remembers the buttery between 1936 and 1940:

The Buttery was just a single counter about four meters long with bar stools in front of it, serving tea, coffee and cakes. It was only small but attractively lit, whilst behind that was a huge restaurant with a stage on which a small orchestra played for afternoon teas and for dinners and so forth.'

Both places were equally as popular as either cinema or theatre presentations. In the buttery, staff members often underwent a daily inspection prior to opening to serve the public. Customers were charged 6d for tea or coffee, quite a lot when the price of a tram was only 1d. Often customers would come down to Cardiff for the day and have a 'cuppa' at the Capitol before wandering off shopping and returning later for a cooked meal prior to a train journey home again. It was a place that held magical memories for many. D.H. Jones enthuses:

I remember with great affection being taken by my mother in the early 1940s to the cinema, preceded by afternoon tea of toasted tea cakes and fancies in the Capitol restaurant. I think I was more impressed with the restaurant, which I considered very posh. What with its comfortable wicker chairs, and the customers who, largely, we would describe today as the blue rinse brigade.'

It was back then that Mrs E. Scuibba, of Gwent, was employed as an usherette and later as a waitress.

Capitol staff members party, 1938

The hub and bub of all that was really exciting. I can recall feeling I was really helping in some small way in the war. There were so many different soldiers, passing through, of all nations. I felt quite proud to have been there at the time.

Situated on the first floor and measuring a total area of 74ft x 50ft, it also incorporated a raised platform space for the orchestra to be accommodated. '[It was] managed by a Mrs Grant,' recounts Mary Grant of Rumney. Mary lived at the rear of the Capitol Theatre during the war years and, a little later, she visited the theatre often and continues, 'She was a very gracious lady, and a supervisor called Miss Probert was there too. The Chef, who seemed to have a French background was one Edmund Veryard of Pontcanna'.

Capitol Trailers

'When I was a teenager, I paid for myself and current girlfriend to go to the Cap'. Being a gentleman, I offered her one of my Senior Service cigarettes, but she insisted we smoke hers: Carstan Full Strength. I spent the rest of the night watching the film through blurred eyes, and hanging on grimly to a churning stomach! End of romance!' (John Foster)

eleven

*There was an ambience about the building that
no other cinema in Cardiff managed to obtain*

Gordon Jerrett, a visitor to the Cap' in the 1930s

Mr Jerrett used to visit the Capitol along with his three friends, back in the 1930s when the Wednesday matinées were a big favourite for the gang. For 6d, 9d or 1s you were guaranteed a main feature, the news, a Popeye cartoon, forthcoming attractions and, to top it all off, a stage show, which during one memorable week was performed by none other than Gracie Fields. Gordon saw Roy Rogers, the 'King of the Cowboys', present a show on the stage which involved singing and interacting with the audience. Always a showman, the act began with Rogers riding his horse, Trigger, up the steps of the foyer.

This famous American duo would play at two shows there and, during the first, the matinee, Trigger hit his head on a lintel beam whilst being manoeuvred from back stage. Amazingly, for the final evening performance, one member of the cinema staff actually saw the horse lower its head as he clip-clopped onto the main stage! With the combination of his partner George 'Gabby' Hayes and Trigger, Rogers established himself as the leading cowboy star of his day. In addition, following the boom of television in America during the 1950s, he went on to achieve further success by way of his own show. Interestingly enough, after Trigger died, his image was preserved in perpetuity and can now be seen in the Roy Rogers Museum, California.

Of course, Roy Rogers was not the first B Western cowboy star to make an appearance at the Capitol Cinema. Gene Autry, another singing cowboy, who was a big star before Rogers took over his crown after Autry's career was affected by the Second World War. Both Rogers and Autry were at one point ranked in the top ten box-office attractions. Quite an accolade at the time. Autry was a tough, no-nonsense screen hero whose pictures were overflowing with live action and low on the romantic front. This was not to say that he proved unpopular with female audiences, quite the contrary.

Autry and his horse, Champion, came to the Capitol Cinema in the mid 1930s, too. He came to promote his latest film, *South of the Border*, during the Saturday morning children's show. Champion was stabled in a garage at the rear of the theatre, with a personal groom in attendance at all times. After encouraging the horse to dance to music, Autry would manoeuvre Champ into rearing up on to his hind legs to climax their act. Mrs B. Darcy started work at the Capitol in 1936, and recollects the visit well:

> I can still hear the horse's hoofs as they clattered on the stage. Gene looked every bit a star; with a lovely golden tan and the bluest eyes I have ever seen. He drew tremendous crowds to see him arrive in Queen Street in a white, open-top car, dressed in white cowboy clothes trimmed with gold.

Getting out of the theatre proved to be a little more hazardous, but Eva Patterson, who had three spells of work experience at the Capitol, also has a call to remember that day. It was during her day off that Autry's show was taking place during the interval and she had come in especially to see it. This was when Paramount Pictures held the lease of the cinema and ordered that all staff leave the building via the back of the circle area after completing their often lengthy shifts. Eva was told to go to the dressing room where a scheme was hatched to enable Autry to finally exit the building safely after meeting some of his fans backstage. It was agreed to sneak him out of the back of the cinema to avoid confronting the mass of fans gathered along Queen Street. Eva had a brief chat with the famous singing actor and his understudy, who, incidentally, took quite a shine to her. She laughs now upon telling the story of walking down Queen Street accompanied by the latter man, who was wearing his full cowboy outfit: guns and all!

Not surprisingly, such a sight caused quite a commotion with people mistaking him for the real Gene, and following the couple, Pied-Piper-like, around the city centre. The newly-discovered friends agreed that he should change into something a little less conspicuous, only for him to return wearing an even larger cowboy hat. Josephine Thomas also has fond memories of the occasion:

> My sister, brother and I were taken by our father to see the 'stars', when they appeared ... we were so excited. Gene sang songs and Champion was dancing and pretending to die. It was great. After they showed one of his films and when the show was over we went to the back entrance of the cinema where Gene and Champion came out to meet the fans. My brother was delighted when Gene picked him up out of all the crowd of children gathered around and put him on Champion's back. You can imagine he was thrilled, as Gene Autry was his favourite cowboy.

Capitol Trailers

'Capitol service, sir!' In the event of any incivility or insubordination from any member of staff, please report immediately to the manager. (Capitol Programme Booklet, *c.* 1927.)

twelve

There were deep, plush red carpets where your feet sank in to

Mrs M. Lewis, former Capitol worker

When the Capitol Cinema initially opened on Christmas Eve 1921, it did so without the inclusion of a theatre organ, and it would be almost a year until one was installed. The original instrument was built by S.F. Dalladay of Hastings, himself an organist and organ builder, whose company predominantly constructed church apparatus. Although the business had supplied work for other cinemas in Britain, the Capitol project was their biggest commission.

In the opening programme notes from 29 October 1922, Mr Hodge espoused thus:

> This magnificent instrument, the finest and most up-to-date organ in Wales [is] in every way worthy of the magnificent hall for which it has been expressly designed, and one which will prove a source of delight ... to which it will form a valuable adjunct in giving expression to what alone the king of instruments can do ... it leaves nothing to be desired.

The Dalladay organ was a valuable addition to the Capitol and it enhanced both film performances and solo renditions with available effects, including a thunder pedal, cymbals, fire-bell, drums and triangle. Its casework was the same as that of a similar one found in an average-sized church and contained thirty-six

Frank Davidson and usherettes on the Capitol roof, wartime

display pipes, a number of which were at a height of 21m. David Clegg, then a world-renowned organ recitalist at the Winter Gardens in Blackpool, played at the inauguration and was suitably impressed with the diversity available, wrote: 'After opening his most effective organ, beautifully built in detail, good and conscientious workmanship suggesting the work of a musician, I had much pleasure in giving thirteen recitals and so had a rare opportunity of testing it'. Sadly, the coming of talking pictures signalled the end of its particular line and the instrument was used only sporadically after this time.

Being positioned in a box at the right-hand side of the stage (and also at some point situated directly upon the stage), it was removed in 1938 for a visit by Queen Mary and replaced. The Lafleur organ was taken away and sold in 1944 to a Bristol firm after its pipework was deemed to be in an excellent condition and some of its parts reusable for life in other instruments. Accordingly, a Hammond organ was positioned in the Capitol and was used by many visiting musicians and local ones such as George Clissold, Jack Hartland, Danny Jones, James B. Smart

Nell Gwyn (1934), a film shown at the Capitol

and 'that brilliant electric exponent', Fela Sowonde. As ascertained by Steve Dutfield, a duty manager at the now-defunct Capitol Odeon in Cardiff and a huge organ enthusiast, all instruments in 1947 were silenced by Rank and many musicians again found themselves surplus to requirements. By the 1960s things had come full circle, and the Capitol regularly made use of an electronic organ in a decade where live shows were becoming a regular feature. Mysteriously, after the closure of the Capitol in 1978, a long time since the organ there had become un-playable, it was removed, the idea being that its elements could be incorporated in other, organ-less theatres. 'This never happened', concludes Steve in an interview with the author. He did, however, hear of an unproven story that claimed some of its parts were used elsewhere, 'Nobody at Rank knows what happened to it'.

If we can return to the past once again, we will find that Frank Davidson was the resident organist at the Capitol in the mid-1930s and was quite a prestigious performer in the eyes of Cardiff audiences. Whilst also playing at the cinema, his band appeared regularly at local dance halls. 'Uncle Frank', as he was known to the children attending the Capitol's weekly Saturday morning 'Popeye club', was held in high esteem by the youngsters, who would participate in a sing-song before going home fully satisfied after two or three hours of fun, all for the princely sum of 3d.

Mr Davidson was not the only organist to entertain children during this time. Arthur Tovey, of Gabalfa, also used to enjoy the Saturday morning shows and he vividly recalls an 'Uncle Sam' playing the organ there. 'It used to have coloured lights over it, and was just behind the stage and was on a lift, and when he started playing it would rise up to stage level. Uncle Sam would get us to sing 'Underneath the Spreading Chestnut Tree', and get us kids to do the action'. Arthur, born in 1929, went on to be employed as a despatch boy in 1946 by Columbia Pictures, who were based in Dominions Arcade. This particular place housed most, if not all, of the major film distributors including MGM, RKO, General Film Distributors (also owned by J. Arthur Rank) through to 20th Century Fox. Film stock was stored in steel vaults underneath the arcade ready for distribution throughout Wales, the West Country, Devon and Cornwall.

Going back to Frank Davidson, the 1930s was a decade when flamboyant public displays of ostentation were of paramount importance to cinemas like the Capitol, and the dapper-looking Frank appeared very dashing with his dark, slicked-back hair, tuxedo and heavy, dark-rimmed spectacles. 'His was a small band and I think they performed most nights at the Cap', remembers W.R. Simmons, a youngster back then. 'Frank and his drummer, Benny, engaged in wisecracks to one another, and they both came over well to the audience. It was a very entertaining show and I, for one, loved it'.

Another Capitol employee, the late Mrs B. Darcy, continues:

When I first joined the Cap' staff in 1936, there was only a three-stringed orchestra and pianist playing in the restaurant. My first memory of him [Davidson] was playing in the pit during intervals. They took away the pit and Frank started his stage shows when visiting shows stopped coming. When the band broke up, due to call-ups, he played the organ alone. He was a brilliant musician who encouraged the audience to sing-a-long with such songs as Roll out the Barrel & Run, Rabbit Run. When he himself was called up, he went into the Air Force, and Fela Sowande took over the organ.

Fela Sownde

Our final tunesmith of merit to mention in relation is indeed the Nigerian-born Fela Sowande. Fela had previously been one of the resident organists at the Empire Cinema, a grand theatre converted to a cinema in 1933 and itself situated in Queen Street (now the site of a Primark store). He was to replace the RAF-bound Frank Davidson at the Capitol in the early 1940s. Ken Wardle, who worked at both the Globe and Park Hall cinemas, remembers him, 'He wore gold, rimless glasses and a huge grin. He played the organ in a jazz style which was unusual in Cardiff, in comparison with Edgar Lewis at the huge Willis in the Park Hall and Wyndham Lewis (unrelated) at the Empire's Compton organ'. Ken, who spent the best part of his working life as the manager of the Globe Cinema in Roath, is a confirmed organ enthusiast but found nothing of particular interest in the Capitol Organ, 'apart from the console which sometimes appeared in the normal manner rising up from a hydraulic lift from the orchestra pit, sometimes proceeding from the wings to centre stage on a concealed track, and sometimes being un-curtained in a left-hand stage box.'

Capitol Trailers

(Once) when I was standing in a queue inside waiting for a seat, a chap near me collapsed and had an epileptic fit. I rushed to the back of the cinema to get the St John's Ambulance attendant who was always situated in the same spot, everyone else just stood there. Alas, when I got back he had recovered and I had lost my place in the queue!' (A Capitol cinemagoer)

thirteen

Just walking into the vestibule made you feel good.
There was just something so special about the place.

Elsie Dowding, Capitol usherette, 1937-39

On St David's Day 1938, there were 4,000 people packed into the Capitol to catch a glimpse of, and to hear, David Lloyd George address the specially invited audience. The Lloyd Georges were celebrating their golden wedding anniversary on that day, during the period when Paramount Theatres controlled this particular cinema. 'Your week is not complete without a visit to the Capitol', sounded the adverts, but cinema enthusiasts had to wait until 5.30 p.m. before being allowed in to see Ray Milland and Frances Farmer in *Ebb Tide* (1937), which was tantalizingly billed as 'Paramount's thundering saga of the sea!'

Only a couple of months later, another VIP guest visited both the capital city and Capitol Cinema – Queen Mary. Mrs B. Darcy recounts:

I was working as an usherette when she visited the Cap' on 6 April 1938. What excitement that caused. In those days usherettes wore air-force blue uniforms of tunic tops with a large gold bow, trousers, beret hat with white gloves and blue shoes. The reason for her visit was a special show, all-ticket, to be performed by children selected from the valleys and formed into a choir. We, the usherettes, had worked really hard and looked forward to having a close-up view of her. However,

CAPITOL

THEATRE
CARDIFF

AN ASSOCIATE
ODEON THEATRE

FRIDAY, April 23rd
1943, at 7.0 p.m.

THE BAND of
H.M. ROYAL AIR FORCE
(Technical Training Command)

By kind permission of
The Air Officer Commanding in Chief (T.T. Command)

Conductor — Warrant Officer FREDK. A. GALE

In aid of the
MERCHANT NAVY SEAMEN'S CONVALESCENT
HOME

Wartime concert, Good Friday, 1943

at the very last moment, we were told to stay in the background. This was because Queen Mary did not approve of women in trousers. Ironically enough, her own grand daughter, Elizabeth, now Queen Elizabeth, wore them shortly afterwards when she joined the Forces.

Queen Mary entered the theatre by way of a corridor screened off from the public and general auditorium and she made her way to a specially sequestered, flower-strewn royal box. A daffodil colour scheme was incorporated within the interior of the building, with yellow and green curtains complemented by Welsh and English flags. The National Anthem was played by the Cardiff Orchestra Society, alongside representatives from Paramount Theatres mixing with many others. Paramount even built a special stage to accommodate the 500 performers that were taking part in the *Royal Variety Performance*, to fill the space watched by the Queen. The show featured a predominance of Welsh artists, the highlight of which must surely have been the sight of the Treorchy Male Voice Choir, singing whilst dressed in their familiar everyday mining work wear.

Eventually, the public was able to view the flower display in the royal box throughout that week and film presentations recommenced that same evening. The theatre had been closed up until 5 p.m. during the course of Queen Mary's visit, taking place in aid of the Glamorgan County Nursing Association and the Cardiff branch of the Queen's Institute of District Nursing. Queen Mary had earlier visited the National Museum and Cardiff Castle prior to her attendance at the matinée concert.

Still in 1938, the original Associated British Cinemas (ABC) chain was the largest cinema circuit in the United Kingdom, with 474 cinemas nationwide. By the mid-1930s, investment and development in the cinema industry was blossoming. J. Arthur Rank had bought into the second-largest chain, Odeon, in 1938, and by 1940 the Capitol would switch from being a Paramount Theatre to an Associated Odeon Theatre.

On Friday 1 September, all of Wales held its breath as the front page of the *Echo* reiterated: 'The world today was still awaiting a response to the demarches which France and Britain handed Germany last night ...' Both countries demanded that the German aggression in Poland should cease, but as we all know Germany made no response and consequently on 3 September, war was declared. Gary Cooper and the Welsh-born Ray Milland were co-starring in *Beau Geste* (1938), which was beginning its second week at the Capitol, in the week that war was languidly announced by the Prime Minister, Neville Chamberlain. The Park Hall was playing *Let Freedom Ring* (1939), whilst the Empire presented a popular Loretta Young picture, *The Modern Miracle* (1939). Hostilities between the countries began almost immediately and, as a precaution, all Cardiff cinemas were closed, 'owing to the severity of war declaration.' With the onset of the Second World War, the environment at the Capitol would have to adapt to the ever changing events occurring across Europe. Again, Mrs Darcy remembers:

When war was declared, we went to work on the following Monday and the manager did not know whether to open or not. He was unable to contact Paramount as the lines to London were blocked; so we all went home. I think that was the only (working) day that the Cap' ever closed. It was business as usual from then on, with people remaining in even during the air raids.

The Capitol Cinema remained open from 10.30 a.m. until 10.30 p.m. during this precarious period and Frank Davidson and his orchestra presented their Sweet Rhythm set between performances three times a day. Cinemas elsewhere reopened on the following Saturday, with the chief constable of Cardiff recommending that all patrons arrive earlier and not take their cars. The Odeon was playing *The Mikado* (1939); whilst the Park Hall had *Laurel & Hardy in Bonnie Scotland* (1935) supported by the latest *Tarzan* adventure. Unusually, all future advertisements for the Capitol were withdrawn and no further ads appeared for quite a considerable number of months. Marcella Dutton, who spent most of her career at the Capitol, recalls:

> The war changed the whole appearance of the place. The foyer of front-of-house was stripped, stair carpet removed, and it was back to all the terrazzo flooring. Scrubbed daily, a central pay desk kiosk was installed, and after the war the Cap' was often mistaken for Queen Street railway station – that's how bare the foyer appeared. We were often asked for tickets to the valley towns at the sweet kiosk, although the station was only around the corner.

The importance that the entertainment business played in bolstering public spirits was underlined within the sentiments expressed in a letter to a local newspaper. A reader extolled the virtues of the place in the times of great 'mental strain'. Fear of night-time air raids led to all Cardiff cinemas having to be closed by 10 p.m. each night during the course of the hostilities. January 1941 saw the heavy bombardment of the Riverside and Canton areas of the city (the suburb of Whitchurch was also to suffer heavily later) and during these years there were around forty major air raids over Cardiff, the last recorded in May 1943. Both the Central and Ninian cinemas kept their films running whilst people, patrons and public alike took shelter inside. The Canton Cinema, Cowbridge Road – now a supermarket – was struck by an incendiary bomb which landed in the main auditorium, but apart from causing a brief, containable fire, thankfully failed to fully ignite. Incredibly, the patrons continued watching the film as all this occurred before them!

In spite of the precarious uncertainty caused by the declaration, consumer choice was aplenty for cinemagoers; with the centrally located Empire, Olympia,

Queen's, Odeon, Park Hall, Pavilion and Central alongside the suburban delights of the Canton, Coronet, Gaiety, Globe, Monico, Ninian, Plaza, Rialto, Splott, Tivoli, Prince of Wales and New Theatres all open for business.

The Capitol Cinema was not the only public amusement centre to suffer the terrors of air raids, as we shall discover. I mentioned in my previous book about Cardiff cinemas, *Ribbon of Dreams*, (ISBN 0946406464, available from the Mercia Cinema Society) how audiences at both the Queen's Cinema, Queen Street and at the Rialto Cinema, Whitchurch Village, were also directly affected by raids.

A truly moving case of the ramifications of war upon the lives of Welsh residents is ably demonstrated by Mrs Josephine Thomas, now living in Bargoed but formerly of Cardiff. In 1941, she visited the Capitol along with her sister and cousin to see the latest film on offer, when an announcement came over the screen informing the audience that an air-raid warning had been sounded. Meanwhile, the film continued to play, but the audience was told that they could leave the building immediately if they wanted or they could remain seated. Shockingly, a total of 160 British cinemas were destroyed by air raids during the hostilities and it does seem odd that people would take their chances by staying inside a cinema once a raid had been instigated. Still, Mrs Thomas and her family elected to leave and her cousin, who lived in a different part of the city from them, jumped on an awaiting bus to make her own way home. 'The next morning we heard that my cousin, her mother and three sisters were all in hospital; their house had been bombed the previous night. Sad to say her eldest sister, aged twenty-one, was so seriously injured that she died a few days later. Just after this sorry time', concludes Mrs Thomas, 'my family were evacuated to Bargoed where we have lived since'.

Beatrice and Leonard Dinham were frequent visitors to the Capitol Cinema and basement dance hall in the early 1940s, and Beatrice was briefly an usherette, chocolate girl and eventually settled as a Capitol cashier from 1941-48. She recalls a rumour that was prevalent around both the Capitol and Odeon Cinemas which suggested that the latter was going to close and all staff would transfer to the Capitol. Fortunately, this scheme never materialized and today, more than two decades since the old Capitol closed its doors, the Queen Street Odeon remains as strong as ever.

Marcella Dutton spent almost forty years working at the Capitol Cinema after initially starting as a part-time usherette in August 1939:

> Within four weeks, war was declared and I became full-time. Then in 1941 or late 1940 the Tilney family leased the Capitol to Rank/Odeon. I was then in charge of sales and stock, so four of the then staff, including yours truly, went to the Cap' to implement Rank methods. We lost our old boss Oscar Deutsch, who always gave his staff a two shilling Christmas box each year; last time we had one of those!

On another occasion, a Spitfire fighter plane was installed in the cinema foyer. This goes to show the sheer scale of the Capitol. The display was in support of advertising the re-released *Hell's Angels* (1930), itself the most famous aerial drama of the day. Its presence caused quite a commotion with cinemagoers. Two usherettes stood either side of it, dressed in their air-force blue to both promote and bolster the war effort. Consequently, the RAF loaned the female staff their distinguished Glencery caps in a ploy to collect funds for the RAF Benevolent Fund.

The Capitol was rightly nicknamed the 'Welsh Palladium' by many locals when, in the midst of the hostilities, Sunday-night concerts first became universally popular, with many big bands playing there. Leonard Dinham can remember that the Capitol (and the ballroom especially) was packed with Americans during the war and he attended many Sunday concerts, 'It was the first time that I'd seen people Jittebuggin' in the aisles!'

For Gordon Jerrett, visiting the theatre from 1941-43 also proved a rewarding experience:

> I attended quite a number of concerts. The local authorities would allow a concert on a Sunday but stopped films being shown or Good Friday. Hence the advent of the frequent Sunday concerts staged there, almost always sell-outs. I think the prices for concerts started at two shillings and sixpence, quite expensive in those days. The programme, however, itself was free.

To be certain of a good seat, people would start queuing at 6.30 p.m. in anticipation of an evening's entertainment. A typical Sunday concert saw the H.M. Royal Air

Force Band in April 1943, with a selection of Chopin, Mozart and Strauss mixed freely with half an hour of swing, before the finale and *God Save the King*. Things started to change at the Capitol once the big bands and stage shows ceased due to musicians and performers receiving their call-up orders, and only Frank Davidson remained for a little while longer to play the solitary organ.

From the seventeen cinema venues available for the delectation of Cardiffians in 1939, at the end of the war the cinema population had mushroomed to include a further four: the Coliseum (Canton), Avenue and Regent Super Cinemas (both located in Ely) and the County Super Cinema, to be found in Rumney. Rank had close to 650 cinemas in 1945 when annual weekly attendances peaked at 30.5 million with a total of 4,723 screens in the UK.

The Odeon Cinema circuit was sold to J. Arthur Rank in 1941, the same year that its founder, Oscar Deusch, died, and the company profits had reached a little over £1.5 million. Rank had already bought his way into Odeon in 1938, twelve months after the circuit had been made a public company with a share capital of £6 million. J. Arthur had steadily been creating the foundations to his phenomenal business empire from the early 1930s, and had acquired the Gaumont-British circuit of cinemas. At one time, the entertainment mogul controlled three Queen Street cinemas – the Empire, Odeon and Capitol. For a fully comprehensive account of his life, I would heartily recommend a book by Geoffery MacNab, titled *J. Arthur Rank & the British Film Industry* (Routledge, 1993) because, as well as being a key source of information, it is also a rewarding and fascinating read.

With a 'land fit for heroes' promised for the returning men and women from the forces, the traditional Sunday shows returned with a vengeance. Owen Martin, now a Rumney resident, remembers:

For us youngsters, the Capitol came to life about two hours prior to the programme when we would be queuing outside, along Queen Street and into Churchill way. I think the prices were 2s 6d downstairs, 3s 6d in the balcony. When I think of it! Ted Heath in his blue suit and brown suede shoes, Dickie Valentine, Lita Rosa – what a show! The girls would be dancing up and down the aisles, all clapping our hands, by today's standards very orderly, and when the vocalist came on, he or she had our undivided attention.

fourteen

Float like a butterfly, sting like a bee. I am the greatest!
Muhammed Ali

Indeed, for many youngsters and adults alike, Ali was the greatest, if not fighter, then certainly one of the great showmen of his generation. In the times before satellite broadcasting and pay-per-view took boxing away from the ordinary fans, the Capitol Cinema was the place to be if you wanted to see the latest Ali bout in the late 1960s and the early 1970s. His most recent fight would be beamed live via satellite and projected onto a 6ft x 4ft screen for the 3,000 people crammed in to each and every seat. There would be two or three fights and Ali's previous outing would be screened again prior to the 'big one', which usually came on after 2 a.m. Owen Martin recalls:

They were a tremendous success. I saw most of them with a couple of friends. Many a night, or should I say morning, I went home and put my working clothes on and went straight to work. Some of the shows lasted until 5am or 6 a.m. We would pay about £1.50 for a ticket, seems unbelievable now; but the Capitol was always packed and for some shows there were even men selling their tickets for a handsome profit. Everyone would be trying to say 'Hello' to Joe Erskine and Dick 'The milk' Richardson. Most of the top sportsmen in South Wales would be there, have a couple of beers and talk, but although there was a fair amount of drinking going on, I can't remember seeing any trouble off the screen.

Capitol film and stage advertisement, 1970s

A huge, sprawling bar area replaced the former restaurant at the Capitol and, not surprisingly, it was always overflowing whenever there was the latest Ali fight. For the female members of staff in attendance, the heavy, testosterone-filled air could prove somewhat disconcerting at times. Nevertheless, led by Marcella Dutton, they ably dealt with whatever came their way. More often than not, inebriated fight fans would be incapable of recalling where they were sitting and ended up standing at the back of the circle or stalls. It was in the course of one of Ali's bigger defence fights that mounted police were needed to control the massive crowd, many of whom had purchased tickets but could not enter the building due to the sheer volume of people, both inside and out. 'They started battering all the front doors', Marcella remembers, somewhat disconcertingly. 'The situation was getting out of hand at about 3 a.m., so Mr Hall, our general manager, opened every door at the rear of the stalls so that all those outside could see right through to the screen and it cooled the entire situation, which had been growing angry.'

On a lighter note, Miss Dutton was called to placate a woman in the stalls who had been complaining about the man next to her. Apparently he had been shouting and screaming his way throughout all the preliminary bouts and had become quite a nuisance to those around him. Miss Dutton decided upon evasive action. She borrowed a torch belonging to an usherette and threatened to hit him over the head with it. This quietened the individual down and the other woman then thanked her for succeeding in shutting her husband up!

fifteen

The place was packed with us teenagers
clopping our feet to the beat of the music.
It was sheer joy listening to our Rock & Roll heroes.

Stan Philips, Capitol visitor

Mr Phillips was just one of close to 5,000 fans that attended both of the forty minute shows by the American singer Bill Haley in February 1957. Stan, who now resides in Ely, had paid his first visit to the Capitol shortly after the end of the Second World War, when his mother took him to see *King Kong* (1933). The film caused quite an effect upon the disposition of the delicate seven-year-old, although things were distinctly different when he returned as a teenager to see 'Bill Haley and his Comets', as the 3d *Echo* listed them. Haley was at the peak of his career after having wooed many young Cardiff cinemagoers and caused headline news, with his *Rock Around the Clock* film two years earlier. The rocker stayed at the Angel Hotel, Westgate Street, and had to have a police escort back there after completing his shows.

Tickets to see the 'King Kiss Curl', as Bill was commonly known, generated queues flowing along Churchill Way and as far down as the old swimming baths in Guildford Crescent. The scramble for tickets caused the gigs to be sold out in a little over two hours. The then chief constable of Cardiff, Mr W.F Thomas, had voiced his concerns about the concert in the local press, 'Let us see if Cardiff can behave like a city of culture, art and live music and not stoop to the level of some other towns and cities in the country.' Mr Thomas was clearly not a Haley fan but, if the Capitol Theatre management had had their way, they could easily have sold 10,000 tickets.

'I remember the crowds and the screaming more than anything else,' reminisced one female fan to a local newspaper. Audience members were dancing on their seats as well as in the aisles and the night went down very well. Welsh star Ray Milland could be seen in a film called *Lisbon* (1958) during that week and, whilst the young audience were diggin' the Comets, a special souvenir supplement was available for fans to purchase with the tantalizing by-line of 'You must dig this, you crazy cats!' Not everyone was as hip to the current music scene though, as the following scene which took place that same evening in the foyer will demonstrate.: 'Two for the three's, please' asked the first lady. 'Tickets only.' replied the cashier. 'But isn't Ray Milland here in Lisbon?' came the bemused response, as the movie fan looked firstly at the cashier and then to her friend.

Already enjoying a shareholding in the former Gaumont-British cinemas circuit, prior to its conglomeration into the Rank empire in 1941, 20th Century Fox expected the installation of new equipment in theatres to cope with the demands made by Cinemascope. Other American movie studios had also invested in the remaining British circuits, and predominant in the 1930s were Warner (ABC), MGM, Fox (Gaumont-British) and United Artists (Odeon). Extensive electrical work was necessary to enable the installation of Cinemascope, including fitting stereophonic sound speakers behind the screen as well as around the general auditorium. The Rank family was somewhat resistant but they did go on to equip seventy of their cinemas with the new system. On a national scale, they had not wanted to disrupt their weekly changeover of film programming, with the logic being filmgoers had developed the habit of visiting the cinema weekly, and the company argued that any prolonged variation to this pattern could prove detrimental. Fox had made the subsequent demand for the instigation of the extended run and, of course, with the formidable success of the extensive season enjoyed by *The Sound of Music* at the Capitol in the mid 1960s they would eventually be proved right.

Stepping back into the 1950s, we find the Capitol, still holding on to its ambience of yesteryear with its wine-coloured usherettes' uniform and

Above: Bill Haley *Rock Around the Clock* poster

Right: Bill Haley

the braid-edged, commissionaires' outfits epitomizing the facade. Richard Burton and Jean Simmons were the stars of *The Robe* (1953), the first movie to be released in the new, widescreen, Cinemascope format and presented at the Capitol Cinema. It ran for a month and proved to be so popular that it generated queues both inside and outside the theatre. A total of 40,000 seats were sold on its last week and an astonishing 10,000 people saw the last four performances on its concluding Saturday. They even started waiting to get in as early as 9 a.m. on that final day. *The Robe* was hugely significant because it was the first feature film to instigate a new dimension in film exhibiting in Cardiff – the extended run. What this meant in actuality was simply that a particular film would be shown exclusively in one cinema rather than, as today, when a film such as *Titanic* (1998) played simultaneously at both the ABC and Capitol and Queen Street Odeons. So if you wanted to see *The Sound of Music*, for example, the nearest alternative cinema venue was in Bristol.

Perhaps the supreme example of this new dimension was proven by the massive nineteen month run of *Music*, from April 1965 to November 1966. 'I came in as the second house was finishing and caught the end of the picture, the final scene; and I will never forget the effect of that first sight of the wide screen stretching across the vast stage!' tells cinema enthusiast Derek Creedon, of Canton.

Gwyn Isaac, also a resident of Canton, continues in a similar vein, 'My most abiding childhood memory of the cinema was being taken to the Capitol, from my then home in Tonypandy, to see *The Robe*, on that fabulous wider-than-wide screen with stereo sound – nothing I've seen since has thrilled me so much as a pure cinema experience'. The new sensation of cinemascope, or the 'modern miracle you see without glasses' was a technique actually developed in the 1920s, involving the use of special lenses to spread the film image over a more expansive area than normal.

Critics were agreed that *The Robe* was not a great film but there was a sense of optimism that the new technology could be used on greater material. Local film enthusiasts in Cardiff probably enjoyed more the premiere presentation of the second cinemascope release *How to Marry a Millionaire* (1953) at the neighbouring Odeon Cinema. General admission prices at the Capitol back then ranged from 1s 9d through to 2s 4d and 4s 6d. The film was to mark the end of the booming post-war cinema era and, as the accessibility of television was increasing, anything deemed as new or innovative was grabbed at by the exhibitors. For Stan Phillips, it did not matter, the effect was still memorable, 'As the premier Rank cinema in Cardiff, the Capitol always got the biggest and best films first. I still recall my wonder upon seeing it. As the curtains drew back to reveal the newly installed screen, there were gasps of sheer wonder at its size.'

Above: Tickets

Right: Capitol film listings

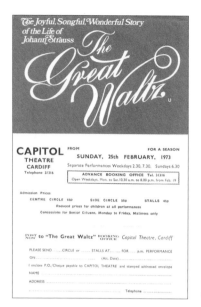

Capitol film advertisement

After the excitement caused with the visit to the Capitol by Bill Haley the year before, 1958 turned out to be an equally incident-packed period at the Queen Street cinema. The installation of a new modern projection system, Todd–AO, at the considerable cost of £4,000 generated a great deal of enthusiasm by Cardiff cinemagoers. The new projectors were regarded in the trade as being the *crème de la crème* of cinematic equipment. The musical *South Pacific* (1958) was the first film to run on the 70mm, widescreen format. Fact fans will know that the system used a six-track sound system, the forerunner to the now familiar Dolby stereo.

With the arrival of cinemascope at the Capitol, Derek Creedon, a certified cinema buff, explains that Rank and 20th Century Fox (the originators of cinemascope) had a major falling out that came about after Fox had announced that all their future film production would be in cinemascope and thus demanded extra running time for each film. It seems ludicrous now, but Rank refused and consequently lost all Fox films for the next five years to an independent chain represented in Cardiff by the Park Hall Cinema. Creedon concludes, 'It was not until 1958 that the breach was resolved, and the Capitol showed *Peyton Place* (1957) and the blockbuster musical *South Pacific*.'

Mr G.K. Williams, of Whitchurch, and his wife received complimentary tickets for the opening night of South Pacific and here is how he sets the scene of that evening: 'All the cinema staff wore Hawaiian costumes, the usherettes sarongs and, prior to taking our seats, the auditorium was sprayed with a heavy perfume. It was quite magical.'

Just as 1945 had seen the dreaded Entertainment Tax brought in by the post-war government, resulting in both the Empire and Capitol Theatres struggling to survive, the Government Tax of the late 1950s equally affected cinemas. It ceased in 1960, when it proved no longer advantageous for live music to be a part of the bill and, consequently, organists across the country lost their jobs. However, prior to this time, the Capitol management were a little savvier in finding ways around the new tax on seats. For a live performance it was possible to get the tax back and so what they did at the Capitol was, prior to a screening of *South Pacific*, there would be a thirty-minute music recital. Unfortunately, this meant that somebody had to be up in the rafters to place a spot light on the soloist, a frequently dangerous job, with the large bulbs having to be replaced and dropped in to a bucket of cold water next to whoever did the job. One person that did this many times, was the late Harry Smith, a second projectionist at the cinema for a great many years, his slim build meaning that, in later years, he was the only person who dared go up there, such was its precariousness.

South Pacific ran for twenty-six weeks throughout one of the hottest summers then on record, 'If it had been a normal summer', said the late Mr W.A.C. Hall, in 1978, 'it would have run all year.'

The Capitol was alive with the sound of Julie Andrews as a singing nun in *The Sound of Music* and it came to be an astronomical success with cinemagoers in the city when it ran there from April 1965 until November 1966. One person, Myra Franklin, saw the film 864 times, 'Since I started', explained the then-forty-seven-year-old Myra, 'I've gained in patience, understanding and love.' The daily routine of the Llanrumney Cinema fanatic was documented as thus: she would leave her home at 1 p.m. and, after arriving in Queen Street, she would have lunch in the cinema café, followed by attending the first show. This was then continued with tea in a local café (the Capitol's, of course) after which she would go for a stroll and return, refreshed and ready for the 7 p.m. screening. Just what the appeal was for Mrs Franklin is anyone's guess, but her adoration for the film landed her with a mention in the *Guinness Book of Records* and a free pass from the cinema management. She always sat in the same seat at the Capitol.

Toratora film-flyer promotional leaflet, 1971

Seats in the circle area at the Capitol in those days cost 10s 6d and 8s 6d, whilst the stalls were 7s and 5s 6d. There were also concessions for children and pensioners. Meanwhile, prices at the neighbouring Olympia ranged from 7s 6d up to 15s, and the prices of admission at the Park Hall were from 5s to 10s 6d. The latest hit record by The Beatles, *Ticket to Ride*, was at the top of the hit parade and comedian Benny Hill was starring in his own show on television. A robust choice of cinemas consisted of the ABC, County, Gala, Globe, Monico, Ninian, Olympia, Park Hall Cinerama, Plaza, Prince of Wales and the Regent all offering the latest choices of the moving image across the city. The 1960s saw the Capitol establishing itself as the home of the historical epic, including *Spartacus* (1960) and *El Cid* (1961) but it was *The Sound of Music* that became the latest and greatest box office hit since *Gone with the Wind* (1939). For the premiere of the now-perennial Christmas-time television favourite, *Spartacus*, muscularly clad gladiators lined the staircase and balcony areas to greet guests as they arrived to see the film.

sixteen

The Tilneys say 'adieu'

A ticket for the circle cost 10s 6d or 8s 6d and 7 or 5s 6d for the stalls at the Capitol in the 1960s. The cover price for an *Echo* was 4d. Annual weekly attendances were in decline as the decade progressed. 9.6 million visited British cinemas in 1960 and the figure decreased to 4.1 million by 1969 with a little over 1,500 screens nationwide. Despite this, British exports were at an all-time high. Associate British Cinemas (ABC) held a lease to the Olympia Cinema, Newport, until its expiry in 1964 although Tilney's Kinemas Ltd, the owners of the cinema, took advantage of an escape clause allowing them to renege on their contract with ABC.

The Tilney family had owned the Olympia since its opening back in July 1912 and the company were in the process of selling off all their cinemas when Chesterfield Properties Ltd bought the site in 1962. Chesterfield Properties Ltd, a London-based business, was prominent in the development of office and shopping schemes throughout the country when they bought the Olympia for £50,000 for redevelopment purposes. Their acquisition of the Olympia Cinema signalled the closure of the sixth picture house in the Newport region since the war. The sale of the Tilney-owned cinema immediately cast a shadow over the future of the Capitol, in Cardiff; of which they owned the lease. 'I have heard nothing about a sale', informed Mr G.P. Bird, general manager at the Capitol. 'It is news to me.'

It was not possible to purchase the freehold to the Capitol and, with the lease running down, it was a commercial necessity to sell up. With developers succeeding in purchasing the Olympia, it was possible to pay out lump sums of money to shareholders out of capital rather than through income, as is common today. It was widely forecast that this loophole was going to be closed by the government and, consequently, it was decided to wind up Tilney's Kinemas Ltd, enabling a large dividend to be distributed to family shareholders. After the death of Ernest's brother, Harold, his sister Cicely, who was immensely fond of her brother, grew desperate and mistakenly gave shares in the family company to her children, Richard and Angela. This shifted the control of the company into the hands of the Tilney children. Subsequently, a power struggle developed to avoid the youngsters keeping possession or being able to strip the company of its assets. Miss Tilney petitioned for the company to issue shares at a nominal value of £1 each to herself and others with the premise of purchasing those outstanding and thus shift the balance of power back to the former board. Richard, Angela and Ernest's adopted daughter, Joan, took their claim to the High Court to have this annulled, and, coupled with the new legislation, they decided to sell their shares. Under the Companies Act (1948), Tilney's Kinemas Ltd went into voluntary liquidation, with receipts from the previous year totalling £354, 629. The company was finally wound up in August 1965.

Cicely, sister of Ernest, was quite a character according to Julian Dolman, himself the son of Beatrice Dolman (née Tilney), sister of Ernest; and married to Arthur Dolman, a managing director of Tilney's Kinemas. Born in 1880, Cicely was a gifted musician who instigated the incorporation of a Palm Court orchestra at the Capitol and it was her idea to position a sweet kiosk at the cinema. Selling tobacco and sweets, the kiosk was positioned just outside the theatre, aimed to generate additional revenue by enabling customers to purchase goods without necessarily coming into the cinema itself. A spinster, she seemed to shrink in size as each year passed, and she regularly had lunch at the Continental Restaurant, situated next to the Capitol Cinema, whilst also maintaining an office in Newport. Cicely lived until 1972 and was ninety-two when she died.

So it was that the Tilney family severed their long standing association with the Capitol Cinema.

seventeen

The rage of Cardiff

1920s Capitol slogan

Having been at Number One in the music charts with *Day Tripper*, The Beatles came to Cardiff in December 1965, as a headlining group in their own right. Their one-time media rivals, The Rolling Stones, also played the Capitol during the sixties but it was the fans of the 'Fab Four' that were screaming, shouting and standing on their seats for the whole duration of the 12 December show. Fanatical fans constantly swamped the lads whenever they played and during the course of their 1965 show, (the group had also been on the bill at the Capotp; back in May 1963) a man jumped upon the stage and grabbed at guitarist George Harrison. George, it seems, was fine but I wonder what he made of his pink-sweater clad attacker on that evening?

Whatever he thought will never be known because as soon as the band came off the stage they clambered straight into an awaiting ambulance, incognito, for a rendezvous at St Mellon's, at which point they jumped into a car and made off to the next venue, all of which took place whilst the crowd at the Capitol were still shouting for encores. I vividly remember that Leslie Priestley, an avid Beatles fan at the time, paid £20 for the Capitol's stage floorboards at a sale of artefacts shortly before the prolonged demolition of the cinema ensued in January 1979. His photograph appeared in the press with Leslie, Cheshire-cat grin exposed, pictured standing next to his treasure. In the same sale, the old Capitol clock was sold.

Another 'Capitolist', Mr Paul Sutton of Barry, always looked forward to the frequent double-bill feature programme that played at the Capitol, sometimes consisting of two James Bond films or a Bond coupled with one of the classic 'spaghetti' westerns of Clint Eastwood. Mr Sutton recounts:

> When Ken Russell's film Tommy (1975) was showing, I can remember walking past the Capitol entrance and hearing very loud music. The doors were fully opened and speakers had been put up in the foyer playing the soundtrack music to such a level it would put some of today's car stereos to shame. You could almost believe walking into the foyer and finding Roger Daltrey stood there singing.

Over at the ABC Olympia in December 1965, Elvis was starring in *Harem Holiday* and Beatles-clones, the Dave Clark Five, were playing in their own film, the quirky *Catch Us if You Can*, projecting at the County Cinema, Rumney and Regent Cinema in Ely. *The Sound of Music* was back for a Christmas season at the Capitol and would continue to enrapture audiences through to November 1966. There was bingo at the Coliseum Cinema, Canton, with a 'snowball' jackpot of £150 offered to the numbers game enthusiasts. Meantime, the Park Hall Cinema was offering its current feature of *The Greatest Story Ever Told* (1965).

The Capitol thrived upon live acts and anybody who was touring the country in the 1960s and 1970s would include a date there, from Rod Stewart to Elton John to Status Quo or Bob Dylan. It was the venue to play in Wales and Welsh audiences were known to be highly vociferous and provided an excellent welcome to visiting performers. In fact, it was not at all uncommon for contractors to be called in the day following a concert, to repair the front rows of seating that were repeatedly torn apart by raucous audiences. The glass in the beautiful panelled doors at the back of the main auditorium would vibrate as a result of the sheer volume and energy generated by the live shows. Stan Fishman, now president of the Cinema Exhibitors' Association, worked for the Rank Cinema circuit for almost thirty years and he was involved with the booking and presentation of live shows at cinemas across the country, one of which was the Capitol. According to a 1960s stage directory published by Rank Theatres Ltd, the Capitol had a seating capacity of 2,492 with very

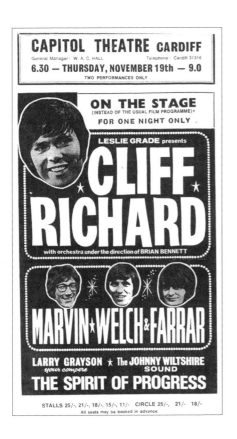

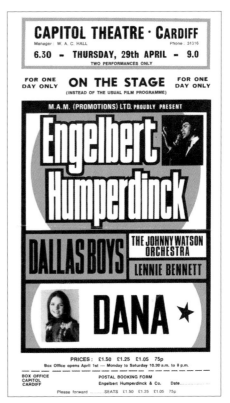

Above left: Cliff Richard concert

Above right: Engelbert Humperdink concert, 1970s

Right: Des O'Connor concert

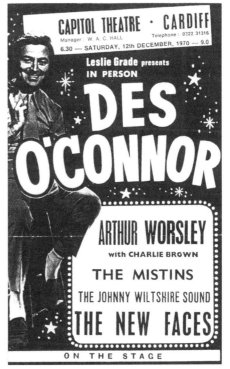

The Mikado film advertisement   *Scrooge* film advertisement

limited stage facilities, such as a stage depth of only 10ft and a width, wall to wall, of 60ft. The proscenium opening was 74ft x 25ft. There were seven dressing rooms, in various states of decoration. There was no stage grid from which to hang stage settings, just two rope sets from which you could hang some backing drapes. Remarkably, it is against that background that the Capitol was in the forefront of the one night concert business throughout all this time. I think that most of us will always immediately associate Sophia Gardens as the home of wrestling, as I remember many evenings with my father there in the 1970s especially, but during a similar period, Stan mentions that even the Capitol tried its hand at staging some bouts in the mid-1960s.

After the Beatlemania phenomenon of the 1960s, the following decade would see Marc Bolan & T Rex, The Sweet, Mud, Slade and Gary Glitter storming both the music and fashion scene under the 'glam rock' banner. There was also to be a far more sinister threat to swarm the country in the early 1970s; a tartan terror called The Bay City Rollers. The group were at the peak of their fame, with two Top Ten albums and two number-one singles, when they brought mayhem to the Capitol Theatre on 20 May, 1975. 'The Rollers' played to an audience that mainly consisted of ecstatic, female fans ranging from ten to fifteen. The ensuing chaos resulted in forty fans singing *Bye Bye Baby* whilst on their way to hospital, victims of nose bleeds, sprained ankles or sprained wrists. 'Terrifying!' shrieked the *Echo* by-line on the following day of the concert, as St John's volunteers told of their fears for the collective safety of everyone who attended the gig. 'The kids wrecked the front rows and I was glad to get out of the place', bemoaned one startled helper. Just as the band had finished their second number, the police stormed the stage for ten minutes attempting to quieten down the screaming crowd.

The gig replaced a screening of the Peter Fonda feature, *Dirty Mary, Crazy Larry* (1974) that played at the Capitol that week, with the price of admission being 80p and 65p. The Plaza, Prince of Wales, ABC and Monico Cinemas were all also advertising their latest delectations that week. The continued success of concerts like the one played by the Bay City Rollers in the 1970s and others, often three per week in the winter, was what kept the Capitol operational. 'The queues usually started the night before the box office opened and during the night were added to by the time we arrived for work at 10 a.m. next morning. They used to cheer when they saw us coming as it meant their wait was almost over,' concludes one former Capitol staff member.

Capitol advertisements, 1970s

eighteen

The wonderful memories of those magical nights in the Capitol

William Rollins, a patron in the 1950s

Film fare presented at the Capitol Cinema in the 1970s included the latest entries in the James Bond series, with *Diamonds are Forever* (1971) and *Live & Let Die* (1974) especially successful, the latter film being an exceedingly popular choice with Cardiff cinema enthusiasts. Stephen King's *Carrie* (1976), *The Missouri Breaks* (1976) and the controversial Dustin Hoffman/Susan George feature *Straw Dogs* (1976) all flickered across the vast screen, to dwindling audiences. The interior steadily deteriorated over the prevailing years and for many people it was all too much. Staff members were aware of the changes and problems on a daily basis. One former staff member offers:

> Television and video came in and cinema audiences gradually decreased. It was much too large for small audiences [by now 2,492 in the circle and 1,484 in the stalls], the ambience of earlier years was lost in the vast hall. Only Bond films did well, but it never filled completely even with those. Heating was a problem, heat was soon lost with a small amount of patrons, consequently it was quite cold on occasions to sit in such a massive hall: very off-putting. It was popular because you were fairly sure of getting in even for the very best of films; I can't remember turning people away for movies.

Mrs B. Darcy returned to the Capitol sometime after she and her husband had moved away from Cardiff and she was startled at the visible change:

The buttery was gone altogether, and the restaurant was a dimly-lit, bare room, not a chair, just a makeshift bar at the end of it; gone was all the glamour. The usherettes were much older than my day. Gone were the uniforms; I left there feeling very sad at what I had seen and never went again. I would rather have my own memories of the place as it used to be.

Things change, business has to progress and adaptability is necessary, if survival is to be grasped. The writing had been on the wall for the Capitol for some time. The crumbling interior was not the primary factor responsible for the demise of the building. It would be the ancient heating system that would prove that the place was financially unviable, within its present context, for Rank. They had announced the planned closure of the cinema in October 1977 but even they had an agenda of their own. A once modern, state-of-the-art system so mutually applauded by the Tilney company and local press back in December 1921, was now proving impossible to run and maintain efficiently. It was constantly breaking down and even the chief area maintenance engineer for Rank confidentially conceded that the whole system needed to be removed. This would have been a vast task to undertake, although this was only one aspect of the maintenance area that needed to be addressed. Put simply, the Capitol had become an expensive white elephant for Rank. Miss Marcella Dutton succinctly summarizes the reality, 'The place was falling apart, which we, who worked there, had noticed already: no surprise.' Running the Capitol was an expensive business for Rank, with maintenance to sustain the heating system proving costly. The problem was that the boiler, located outside in a separate building, had to pump steam to the radiators inside and was often proving problematic.

This was painfully demonstrated when a group called The Spinners played a concert at the theatre in the 1970s. One member of the band was left on stage to sing a solo number but just as he was introducing it to the audience, there was a loud bang from one of the radiators at the side of the stage and, when he again continued, the radiator on the other side also vocalised its distress. 'I'm not gonna do this number. I'm gonna do it later,' conceded the singer.

Curiously, the Capitol was considered a little down market for orchestra recitals and was regarded more favourably for the presentation of rock concerts whereby audiences could really let loose. Rank Theatres Ltd, which contained the national Odeon cinema circuit, had adapted a policy of twinning many of their cinemas in the 1970s along with the introduction of bingo in many of their draughty, old halls. Both the Splott and Gaiety Cinemas in the city had by then successfully adapted into Top Rank bingo clubs and plans were in existence to change the Capitol into a grand bingo club, creatively titled Capitol Bingo. 'There is no doubt in my mind that Rank deliberately (in the 1970s) programmed unprofitable material there to make it obviously unprofitable as a cinema and therefore a potential bingo venture', alleges Gwynn Isaac.

Whatever, the final years at the Capitol were commonly hailed as being very disheartening, with the grand old place frequently only full to a third of its capacity. 'So many of its features reflected the pits end of the era,' adds a second Capitol enthusiast.

Stan Phillips also laments its fatality, 'It was a great loss to the city ... never again to make a date by saying, 'Meet you under the clock at the Capitol steps.' In 1974, Rank offered the Capitol Cinema for sale at between £300 and £400 and Lord Mayor of Cardiff, Albert Huish, met with city council architects to discuss the possibility of purchasing the building. It was considered a possible venue which, located in the heart of Queen Street, could become a exceptional home for the Welsh National Opera (WNO). However, as Mr Huish, now resident in Rumney, imparts, 'Council leaders of all political parties failed to understand the benefits not only to the WNO, but also to the possibility of concerts by international artists.' Regardless of the fact that two teams of architects had prepared feasibility plans for the adoption of the cinema building as a concert hall, facilitating both ballet and opera, it would never materialize. 'Contained in the final plan', concludes Huish, 'was shown an extension of seating from 1,600 to over 2,000, an extension of the orchestra pit, and an added 40ft to the rear of the building'.

The 1974 proposed scheme was well received by those primarily concerned with finding a suitable home for the WNO and enabling Cardiff to be in the spotlight on an international platform. Unfortunately, the Conservative-led council rejected it in favour of building St David's Hall, costing the city £14.5m. 'Why was such a fine building left to disintegrate for the sake of a very expensive inferior one?' questioned one former Capitol-goer in the local press. Founded in 1945, the renowned WNO had consistently struggled to survive due to insufficient funding by the Welsh Arts Council. However, back in April 1946, optimism was running high with the first performance by the newly-formed company premiering at the Prince of Wales Theatre in St Mary Street. The cost for patrons on that night was 3s (pit), 3s 6d (upper circle), 4s 6d (centre stalls), 6s (dress circle) and 6s for the stalls.

A second conducive study was conducted in 1976 by the Cardiff-based architects, Fry & Hughes, and some interesting facts were revealed. It was observed that the full potential of the building was not being, pardon the pun, capitalised upon. The stage in the sweeping auditorium was rightly regarded as providing much flexibility and the proscenium was equally flexible, enabling its width and depth to be increased or decreased for concert usage. The orchestra pit, originally designed to hold up to 120 musicians, which must have been something to see, still had its two lifts enabling a forestage to be conveniently formed at stage level. It was also well known to musicians around the country that the acoustics within the Capitol auditorium were very good. The view was to slightly reduce the volume of sound reverberating, then at 1.5 seconds, which was regarded as high for operatic productions and a little low for orchestral works. An adjustment to the ceiling height and the possible reconstruction of promenade layout was also mooted. The structure of the roof, with its deep lattice girder, acting as an in-between support, was judged as being suitably sufficient to accommodate any scenery girders with hardly any alteration required beforehand. Being over fifty years in operation, all the existing mechanical and electrical heating system was regarded as being far too old and all new equipment was recommended by the report.

An exiting solution was discovered after the WNO commissioned a report that articulated the view that it was clear that the Capitol could successfully be converted into a multiple-use theatre and still screen films. Two minutely differing proposals were put forward. The first provided for opera facilities with seating for 1,768 and concert facilities with 1,938 seats. The stalls, circle and upper circle with extra areas proposed for concerts would be utilized. The second contained an additional idea to make us of the stalls, three circle levels, side boxes and balcony, with additional space for concerts. The seating capacity would be 1,718 for opera productions and 1,888 for concerts. Brian

McMaster, general administrator for the WNO remained distant, 'It (the report) is simply intended to demonstrate that such a conversion is possible. It is not intended as a blueprint for the actual rebuilding.'

All renovation and rebuilding costs were estimated at costing £3.2 million, excluding the additional purchasing fee of the Capitol building itself. What the scheme did indicate was an interesting initiative that should have been put into effect, but there was a problem – where would the necessary funding have been found to turn the dream into reality? This was the major crux of the matter and the grant-maintained WNO publicly acknowledged that financial support would have to be forthcoming from central government, the city council and private sectors. Regretfully, both the Welsh Arts Council and Minister for the Arts, Lord Donaldson, proved powerless to help and the entire strategy collapsed. Lord Donaldson conceded in the *Echo* that the government was resolutely incapable of funding the scheme:

> We are talking in the region of between £4 and 5 million for the Capitol building. I believe it should become an opera house and concert hall one day, and I would simply love to say it could be done. But it is impossible ... it would be wrong to suggest that the government will be able to find five million for this particular project in Cardiff.

Rank was to substantially lower their asking price for the Capitol after it became clear that financial prudence determined a more substantial benefit being made from the sale if it was below even their own base figure. A secondary stumbling block was incurred after it became uncertain as to whether or not Rank would gut the theatre, after closure, to avoid incurring rate charges. The WNO were banking upon using the remaining seats as part of the implementation of any new scheme. Saving them would therefore incur an additional outlay in an already tight budget speculation.

The Rank Organization, however, would continue to operate the Capitol as a working cinema for a further two years after the Fry & Hughes plan was noted but dropped. With an increasingly insipid selection of films playing at the Capitol, a scheme was proposed to convert the theatre into a Top Rank bingo club and mini-cinema complex. Rank Leisure Services outlined their plans for establishing a 2,000-seater bingo hall located on the balcony area and either two or three mini-screen cinemas on the ground floor, resulting in a reduction of the current seating capacity to a quarter of its previous level. A spokesperson for Rank, commenting on the scheme in 1976, stated that the project would result in a stronger choice of entertainment and film selection being made available to patrons within the city centre.

The spokesperson failed, however, to make explicit the real reason for the change in that the Capitol was in a poor state of repair and incurring heavy losses. The 1970s saw an escalating number of struggling single-screen cinemas converted into what were quaintly described as 'studios' – usually two or three small screens holding 200-300 people in each. Bristol and Cheltenham were two recent examples where this change had been successfully executed. Both were shown that to be financially viable. Supporters of the new studio cinemas argued that it would mean that the Capitol could show less commercial films (although many commented that this was precisely what Rank was already, allegedly, doing) for Cardiff audiences to see. In Queen Street, only the Rank-owned ABC Olympia and Odeon remained as possible alternative choices. However it was left to the Sherman Theatre in Senghenydd Road to occasionally present such films that would not necessarily warrant a mass audience.

Not surprisingly, Rank failed to discuss the shocking lack of design aesthetic value made apparent by the implementation of the new, crude studio cinemas, This rationalization became apparent to anyone visiting the newly-twinned Monico Cinema, Rhiwbina, in the late 1970s. It was left to local people, the paying customers, to voice their own concerns and this they did in the shape of a 400-strong petition. It beseeched the Lord Mayor of Cardiff, Albert Huish, to oppose the application by Rank to the city planning department office and subsequent committee considering the plan. Spearheaded by a Cardiff college lecturer, Mr John Lewis, as well as involving a local branch of the young Conservatives, the collective opposition felt that there was already a sufficient number of bingo venues across the city. Six former cinemas were now wearing their bingo hats in the guise of the past Canton, Coliseum, Gaiety, Gala, Regent and Splott cinemas. Not only that, the likelihood of the Rank-controlled Monico Cinema also becoming a full-time bingo hall was a distinct possibility, with the company making a second application for this to become a new venture for the home of the numbers game.

More disconcerting for some was the fact that the decade saw a dearth of entertainment centres available within the centre of Cardiff. 'We want people to bombard the Capitol with protest letters', urged Noel Smith, chairman of Rumney Young Conservatives. 'Cardiff needs to vastly improve its (entertainment) facilities', he surmised in the *Western Mail,* 'not run them down'. Rank vaguely suggested the possibility of up to twenty live events presented at the Capitol after its transgression, the only other venue for visiting performers back then being the limited New Theatre.

In the era when a ticket for the front circle cost 60p, side circle 50p and stalls 40p, Rank voiced their necessity to make better use of the Capitol if it was to sustain itself. They had secured the former Splott Circuit of cinemas (the old SCC) from Sir Julian Hodge in 1976, under the banner of the Jackson Withers Circuit. Rumour had it that one of its latest acquisitions in the 2 million pounds deal, the Plaza Cinema, Gabalfa, was to replace the Capitol, initially as a second-run picture house but with the scope for it to become a first-run hall. A £200,000 outline plan was submitted by Rank to Cardiff City Council and three screens had been detailed rather than the original two screens that had initially been advocated. Headline-grabbing media coverage both contradicted and conveyed an uncertain future for the Capitol Theatre in the final twenty-four months of its working life, from 'Capitol bingo is on the cards', to 'We just can't let this happen to the Capitol', and finally clarification in 'Bingo plan for city cinemas is thrown out'.

As a consequence of the failure to secure a bingo playing license for either the Capitol or Monico cinemas, the latter was sold to a local businessman in 1977 and ultimately secured its future for the next twenty years. The Monico had been struggling as a working cinema and Rank's predominant interest in mainly the larger profile, high-street located cinemas meant that there was a distinct threat of closure looming over the Rhiwbina-situated cinema (which has now since closed). Incidentally, it was itself twinned in 1978 and prospered from the closure of the Capitol because it was now able to show current film releases earlier by becoming a second-run cinema exhibiting films that had already played the high-street theatres.

The final scene to be played out at the Capitol provided no happy ending, though. City councillors rejected the dual application made by Rank to run both the Capitol and Monico cinemas as bingo halls although, significantly, in the case of the former, the planning department recommended that the submission be approved. Despite a significant public outcry city planning officer, Eurfyl Davies, conceded in the *Echo*, 'From a purely technical assessment of the proposal I cannot recommend that it be refused'. Just a shame about Cardiff losing yet another 'place of amusement' for the sake of commerce. The nominated scheme went to a public inquiry after the revelation that the refusal and subsequent appeal made were equally invalid. This was due to an error resulting in the failure to advertise the Rank project lawfully. Of real significance was that in an uncharacteristic step, the latest Secretary of State for Wales, John Morris, basically articulated that any future application should still be considered, regardless of the resulting inquiry.

So seemingly all of this would have resulted in the survival of the Capitol, right? Emphatically, the answer was 'no'. The decree by the Secretary of State resolutely meant the end of the Capitol Theatre as a working cinema; the only question of any weight now was when exactly the end would come for the cinema. It was not far away.

In the year that saw the Sex Pistols at their most noxious, and streets around the country were reclaimed by the people, for just one day, allowing Union Jack plastic hats to be worn and flags to be waved at street parties in celebration of the Queen's silver jubilee, the Capitol Theatre was also in the spotlight back in 1977 but for all the wrong reasons. 'Rank deny that the Capitol will shut down by May 22', cried the April *Western Mail* headline. It reported that no future live shows were being taken by Rank, remembering that this was their only source of profit for the Capitol, for the forthcoming season. Films were still continuing to be booked on no more than a week-by-week basis. Ominously, this could enable the theatre to be closed down very quickly and with the briefest of notice. John Conlon, general manager at the Cap', told the *Echo*, 'We have said nothing about closing although we have admitted we have a problem and intend to sell. The dates are all speculation. Although there is something in the wind, this would have to come from director level'. So, even senior management at the Capitol itself were not sure of just what was going to happen next, or more succinctly, when it would happen.

Capitol auditorium, 1978

The staging of fifty or so live concerts facilitated at the Capitol each year was its life-force, but with the recently converted upgrading of the Plaza Cinema, Rank now had the luxury of three possible first-run cinemas and, fatefully for the Capitol, two was indeed company and three was most definitely a crowd and as a result, its closure was now a reality. Also detailed by the *Western Mail* was the information that the Welsh National Opera had been offered the Capitol building for a purchase price of somewhere between £400,000 and 500,000. Rank had been attempting to find a buyer for the theatre for quite some time and made no secret of this, the WNO was given an end of May deadline. It proved not to be forthcoming.

Capitol Trailers

Not forgetting 'Mac the Artist': who incidentally always wore an artist's smock like Eric Gill. His studio was on the first floor where there was a large area closed off to the public. Thelma Joslin, who worked at the Cap' during the 1950s, recalls the walls were painted with scenes from the Arabian Nights. Mac's function was to design the forthcoming attractions posters which were then posted at various points throughout Cardiff.

nineteen

Tall, potted palms each side of the staircase,
basket weave settees dotted around and four splendid,
uniformed doormen in white gloves! It was all very imposing.

Marcella Dutton on visiting the Capitol during the 1930s

A double bill of *The Street Killers* and *Yellow Emmanuelle* was the final 'X' certificate show at the Capitol Cinema on 21 January 1978. There was an escalating 1.5 million unemployed and the majority of Cardiffians seemed to stay at home on that evening, probably watching the latest episode of the cultural comedy *Mind Your Language*. Film categorization consisted of four different certificates; 'U' – suitable for general family viewing, an 'A' – children welcome, 'AA' – for people aged fourteen or over only and the 'X' – adult entertainment for over eighteens only. Weekly cinema attendances across Britain had been declining in the 1970s, at the start of the decade totalling 3.7 million, but by 1977 were down to just 2.1 million.

There was a total of 1,547 screens in the UK in 1977 when the Capitol was featured in an advertisement in the 7p *Echo*, alongside the Odeon and Plaza cinemas, with the single sentence, 'This theatre closes tonight' being the unequivocally clear definition of its fate. In Queen Street, the home of so many picture houses, only the former Olympia, now known as the ABC 123 remained as a working cinema. The Monico, Prince of Wales, Globe, Plaza, Chapter, Sherman and New Theatre also offered an additional choice of entertainment on that last night. Indeed, an additional entry, the Monroe Cinema situated on a part of the former Globe Cinema, itself closed in late 1998 becoming a victim of the multi-screen traffic jam within the city.

Going back to after the 8.35 p.m. performance of *Yellow Emmanuelle*, cinemagoer Bryan Booth, 'walked around the theatre to the noise of the banging pipes and very few people for the final curtain'. He spent many happy moments at the Capitol and saw all the big bands and a great number of music concerts in the days when 'everything about the Capitol was immaculate.'

Another visitor to the Capitol at around this time was W.R. Simmonds, who returned with his family after a long time away, to see the star-studded reissue of *The Poseidon Adventure* (1972). 'I was shocked when I entered the cinema. It was cold, half full and had a general air of decay', outlines Mr Simmonds. 'What struck me most was the state of the lavatories, which were always in pristine condition. It made me a little sad.'

A further significant reason for the closure of the Capitol was the fact that cinema audiences were in a steady, if fluctuating, decline and would go on to reach their lowest ebb in 1980, with just 1 million visiting each week. This figure may not read as being anywhere near troubling to you or I, but when compared to the 26.8 million in 1950 or 9.6 million of 1960, it makes for disturbing reading. Outside of the school holidays, admissions at the Capitol were poor. Some films were the exception to the prevailing rule – the latest Roger Moore outing as James Bond in *Live & Let Die* swelled daily attendances to a fantastic 9,000 per day and the film had a tremendous opening week at the theatre. Just like many other Bond films, this specific 007 cinema release was the top money maker of 1972.

The twinning and tripling of single-screen cinemas in the late 1970s saw the Queen Street Odeon and the Monico Cinema both becoming examples of the new trend. The late W.A.C. Hall, a much-loved, former manager at the Capitol, added his views about the closure and commented that it was a waste to let the Capitol disappear into obscurity. Mr Hall, affectionately known as 'Wacka' by staff members, was installed as the manager at the Capitol in 1950 and remained there until his retirement in 1973. In a 1993 *Echo* feature, Alex McKinty amusingly retells of when the American movie star Danny Kaye visited the Capitol and persisted in renaming Mr Hall as 'Mr Mouse-tash'; in acknowledgement of the

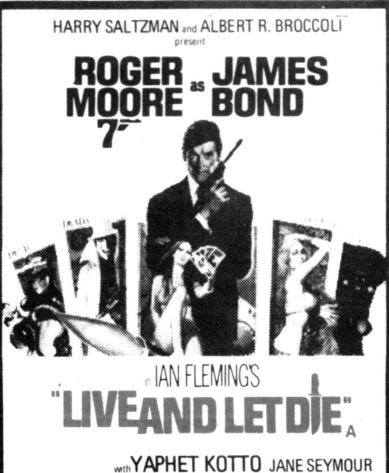

Live & Let Die film flyer

large and dashing moustache that the manager was inclined to wear. 'It was the heyday of the film industry and my father loved being a part of it', enthused Jane Thomas, one of Bill's two daughters, in the article.

The comments made by Mr Hall about the Capitol came immediately after the cinema had closed and some four years before its demolition in early 1982. 'A compromise could surely have been worked out', he said, 'The auditorium really is big enough to be converted into three small cinemas and a 2000 seat concert hall. It could be a superb centre for this city'. Alas, nothing was to happen as a result of his comments and it was even rumoured that Tesco was interested in converting the building into a supermarket. An attempt to turn the place into an arts centre was also spoken of. The Welsh National Opera would have moved into the building if not for the small matter of having to raise £5 million being overcome.

Regrettably, none of these plans materialized and it was the same old story for the Capitol as had befallen many other Cardiff cinemas; the building was boarded up and left to rot. Property all around the Capitol had been sold for redevelopment in 1978 and so Rank found it apt to sell. The company had been in the process of actively selling off all property owned by them outright and holding on to any which they held the lease, which was were the Capitol came. 'It was a lovely place and terrible when it went but it was a bit of a dinosaur', surmised one former deputy manager. The fact that the Capitol was situated in the commercial heart of the city meant that it was visibly allowed to die an undignified death that was to linger until the early months of 1982. Those who had most to gain labelled it an eyesore and I can remember glancing up at part of the supporting walls that remained for a time after the main demolition had been concluded. Segments of its original framework remained in place, forlornly looking out onto Queen Street; as an irreplaceable reminder of what once was. A lost outline of a stairwell now leading nowhere, could be glimpsed if any of the local shoppers bustling about were to have looked upwards.

The entire block of small shops alongside the Capitol all made way for a new shopping centre and the space occupied by the Capitol itself, was prior to this, used as an NCP car parking lot. Parts of its neighbouring building would remain in use as a cheap junk store, before the whole area was flattened. Even then, the Capitol put up a struggle, the strength of the building never being in doubt. Rank eventually sold the site in 1979 and it was purchased by the Guardian Royal Exchange Assurance group for redevelopment. A number of Capitol staff members went on to work at the Queen Street Odeon (also controlled by Rank) and some accepted voluntary redundancy. 'There was always a great atmosphere working there', recounts Wendy Brown, of Whitchurch. 'We had good times, I started at the Capitol in 1965 as an usherette, selling ice cream or programmes, also there was a sweet kiosk which I worked. They (Rank) were a good firm to work for, very fair.' Market research carried out at the time showed that any new development built upon the former cinema site would have to contain the name 'Capitol' because it was still synonymous with the area and in the minds of local people. Therefore, the new shopping complex was to be called 'The Capitol Exchange.'

Public reaction in the months leading up to the demolition of the Capitol Theatre and the neighbouring Cory Hall (opened in 1896 and famous for its political meetings and concerts) caused great consternation. Writing in the letters page of the *Echo*, local resident, P. James bemoaned; 'In enlightened areas such places are getting out the gold paint and I believe any panel of conservationists would pronounce the Capitol ... worthy of preservation as

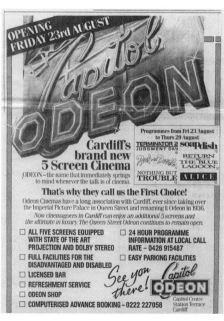

Capitol Odeon film adverts

CAPITOL
CARDIFF

Hello, Dolly!
Matinee 2-30
Doors open 2-4
FRIDAY
MARCH 6
CENTRE CIRCLE
ADULT 12/-
CHILD 6/-

B37

BLOCK B
TO BE RETAINED

Old Capitol film ticket stub

a link in the historical record for Cardiff's posterity.' He was to conclude succinctly, 'It (the Capitol) is unique in Cardiff'.

Guardian Royal Exchange voiced their own response to the rapidly decaying Capitol and Cory in the local press, 'Both buildings have been allowed to deteriorate, but that's by accident rather than design. Portions of the Capitol are very dangerous and the Cory Hall has serious dry rot. We wanted to save both, but it hasn't proved possible.' Planning permission was applied for to the city council, with the group decreeing that both properties would be demolished as part of the redevelopment of their owned land in Queen Street, Station Terrace, North Edward Street and Churchill Way. A further scheme titled Queensgate was rejected by the local authorities after going as far as an appeal in the High Court. The city council did, however, approve the amended plans submitted by Guardian Royal Exchange, after changes included the incorporation of up to six cinemas – two at ground level and a further four at an upper level.

With progress having been made, plans were conducted to dispose of the internal fixtures and fittings and a sale of its contents took place in January 1979. (Although curiously in a *Cardiff Journal* article in January 1980, a mention is made of an additional sale). Cooke & Arkwright, Chartered Surveyors, organized the sale on behalf of the new owners and the accompanying catalogue information included the following advice to prospectors or nostalgia enthusiasts: 'Owing to the difficulties with parts of the lighting within the theatre we respectfully suggest that prospective purchasers attend the viewing equipped with a torch.' Divided up into nineteen independent lots, the bones to be picked over encompassed everything from velvet curtains, tables and chairs, fire hoses, exit signs and row upon row of seats (nearing 2000) which I believe ended up in the now-closed Monico cinema. Three grand pianos were also for sale; the first being a Schiebayer that had languished on the left side of the stage area, a second was located in the balcony to the right of the stage, and a third, had formally been in use in the ballroom. However, he item that caught most attention was the last lot, number nineteen, the Capitol clock. I have often wondered if perhaps even now, if it is lingering in a hallway or lounge somewhere in Cardiff, no longer gazed upon by anticipating eyes.

The Capitol Exchange Shopping Centre commenced business in November 1990, with a combination of shops, food outlets, kiosks and on-site parking facilities for up to 500 vehicles. Construction work on the site of the former Capitol began in October 1987, with the architects underlining their Victorian design as being influenced by the tradition for arcades prevalent in Cardiff since the turn of the last century. The complex was labelled one of the ugliest buildings in Wales by design critic David Petersen and a *Western Mail* headline was also less than complimentary; 'Capital? It's more like toy town'.

All that there was left to do now was to conclude negotiations to allow the erection of the first multiplex cinema venue in Cardiff, as a part of the new centre. Up to ten screens could be included in the new site and competition was heavy. Capitol Exchange project manager, Nick Mason, informed the media of the continuing negotiations with five separate companies; at least three of them seriously so. AMC (American Multicinemas), Maybox and Rank (Odeon) were the main contenders and at one point, AMC, the originators of the multiplex cinema in 1963, came close to winning the contract. A spokesperson for the company acknowledged Rank as being their main source of recognizable opposition. This was in 1988, when the lease to the Queen Street Odeon was due to expire in a year or two, as was the one held by Cannon (the former Olympia and ABC). Maybox, a London-based group, eventually dropped out of the running after their own plans for an eight-screen site came to nothing. Rank, in the form of Odeon, won the race and opened Cardiff's first five-screen multiplex cinema on 23 August, 1992. The Capitol Odeon presented a special charity premiere of the weak Sylvester Stallone comedy, *Oscar*. Former Capitol staff members were invited to the opening night at which not a trace of their old Capitol remained. Only the free-flowing typeface in the word 'Capitol' Odeon logo gave a hint of the past. 'ODEON – the name that immediately springs to mind whenever talk is of cinema' sweetly boasted the press advertisements to publicise the opening of the new cinema. All five screens in the 1,200-seat complex were fully equipped with the latest projectors and Dolby sound system. A grand total of 98 million patrons visited the cinema nationally in 1992, and the multiples had a thirty-one per cent share in the UK screen percentage.

Clearly, the new Odeon did have an effect upon the existing picture houses around, situated next door to the Odeon in Queen Street, in particular shadowed. Admissions there, in the year following, fell by 50,000, yet in spite of the limited distribution of film product available to them, Cannon (once known as the Olympia, ABC and now again as the latter but being independent of its predecessors) increased their audience to 213,000 by 1994. However, the future of the ABC and Odeon Cinemas have subsequently been fixed; they were both demolished to make way for more shops.